Essays

Jack Eden

The American Dream

Introduction

The American Dream has been an inspiration for many people all around the world. It stood for freedom in a world that was governed by fascist, communist, or other dictators; it promised richness in a world where people are starving, are dressed in rags and don't know how they will live next week; it showed a road to a better life that could be taken by anyone; a road that was not blocked by the privileges of a small elite, the aristocracy, that unyieldingly stood in the way and made sure that it's rights were protected while the rights of the people were not worth a dime.

The American Dream promised a better life, it promised Paradise on Earth, it promised freedom to the oppressed – and for many of us it was more than just a promise; it was a dream that became true.

Today, however, it seems that these times are over. It seems that the American Dream is only what is says: a dream, a hope that lingers on the horizon, a promise to the poor and oppressed without any possibility to reach it.

There might still be examples where someone made it from "rags to riches" as the saying goes. But these examples seem to be the exception that proves the rule. At least the impression is becoming stronger that the "land of the free", as it is called in the National Anthem, is only free for a small minority of Americans. Some small elite, distinguished by its wealth from the rest of the Americans, still can live the American Dream. But for the majority of the Americans, however, this dream has turned into a nightmare.

This essay will be a critique of some parts of the American spirit, of the American identity, of the American politics. You might wonder why someone living outside of the USA should bother to criticize America. Are there not enough problems in Europe or Germany? Oh yes, there are. More than just one. And I am not even thinking of the so-called "Euro-crises", which might be the most famous European problem these days in the USA. There are many more problems to talk about.

But in addition to looking at our home-grown problems, looking at America is an important exercise for everyone living in Europe; and probably not only for those living in Europe. Because America is still the largest economy in the world, it is the biggest military power, and it is the politically leading nation. America is not just a country; it is a spirit that formed the modern Western lifestyle. The USA is the trendsetter for Europe and the world. Any political or economical decision that America makes has a direct impact on us.

America is not just Coca-Cola and Walt Disney. It is Google, Amazon and eBay. It is Hollywood and its TV series and blockbusters that fill our cinemas. It is the way we do business. It is the way we look at the world.

America is not only a country across the ocean. It is a dominating part of our politics and economics. It is part of our life. And this gives us to right and the duty to criticize developments in the USA which seem to go in the wrong direction just as we have the right and the duty to criticize wrong developments in our home-country.

Don't misunderstand me: I don't have the intention to criticize America as a whole as some Islamic fanatics and other nincompoops are doing it. As a whole, I like America, its democratic spirit and its openness. Where would Germany be today, if America hadn't intervened in the Second World War and defeated the nazi-government (I know, nazi should be written with a capital N, but I just won't do it)? Maybe we would still be governed by this inhumane and criminal government. Maybe not just Germany, but the whole of central Europe would still be under nazi command. Just the thought of it makes me shiver. I definitely prefer to live in today's American influenced Germany.

Nevertheless, we have the impression that something has gone wrong in America. And it is just about this development that I want to talk in this essay.

The American Dream was a fantastic idea. It was more than just an idea. It was a political program that promised freedom for those that were oppressed by the absolute monarchs in Europe in earlier centuries and by ruthless tyrants all over the world in recent times. It was an economical program that paved the road to wealth for all. In America, every man was the architect of his own fortune. It didn't matter where you had grown up, it didn't matter who your parents were, and it didn't matter to which social class you belonged: You could make it in America. Freedom to live, chances to find a better life, and a true democracy: That's what America meant to the world.

This picture of America, however, is changing. In former times, everyone was better off than his parents. When the new Americans arrived with literally nothing but the clothes they were wearing at the harbors of New York or Boston, they were sure that their kids would lead a better live. They would have their own house, their own car, could afford a good education for their children and maybe even go on vacation once in a while. But now, the younger generations only seem to be worse off. Many hard working Americans lost their homes after the financial crisis and are now living in their cars or on the street. And many of them have lost all hope that it will be better again – or that their kids will have a life that's better than the life of former generations.

Many districts in American cities are now war zones, with crimes rates going up steadily and the police on the retreat, because the citizens have lost their faith in America and are taking the law in their own hands. Almost as many people are killed each year in cities like Chicago and Washington as in the whole of Germany.

There are still places where life is good, where villas worth millions of dollars are changing hands as easily as a package of heroine in the lost quarters. But next to the shining places of the rich are the devastated streets of the poor that look more like streets after a nuclear holocaust as known from so many Hollywood movies.

The American way of life that only went up seems to be going down the hill now for many citizens of the middle-class, with no idea how to stop it.

So one might wonder: What went wrong? Where did America take the wrong turn to get on the street that's leading down?

The explanation is probably not easy, it never is. But to my mind there is one important point that should be considered when finding the answer, a point that seems to be the Holy Grail of America: Freedom at all costs, freedom with no limits.

If someone asks you to define America's core value, it bet you will come up with freedom. Nothing seems to be more important to Americans than freedom (and then: probably nothing is). We want the freedom to choose what we want to do, where we want to live, where we want to work, which job we choose, how we want to live, what we want to say, and so on and so on.

After all, America was formed by those who were looking for freedom, by those who wanted to live their way, who wanted to escape from the oppression of tyrants in their home-countries. These tyrants forbade their citizens to speak their mind or, as an old joke goes, they could say everything they wanted – as long as it was in line with the thinking of their leaders.

Wherever an American believes to detect a restriction of freedom, he revolts against it. It is an inborn behavior, almost an allergic reaction. This reaction, however, helped to establish democratic societies in many countries around the globe. We cannot worship it highly enough.

But then we might ask a heathen question: Can there be too much freedom?

Having a lot of something is often a good thing. And we don't have a problem to understand that there can be too much of some things. Too much to eat will lead to obesity which is bad for your health and might lead to an early death. Too much alcohol is also not good for your health. Too much poison in your veins will kill you, although a small amount of it might heal you. As the physician Paracelsus once put it: "All substances are poisons; there is none which is not a poison. The right dose differentiates a poison and a remedy."

But is this also true for freedom? Can too much freedom be dangerous? This rather sounds like an oxymoron, a contradiction in itself.

However, we shouldn't judge too quickly. There might be more to it than meets the eye.

In this essay, I am trying to explain, why there really can be something like too much freedom – and why too much freedom can be dangerous for a society.

The executive summary for this seemingly nonsensical statement is very short: Too much freedom means no rules at all; everyone can do as he likes. But no rules at all doesn't mean absolute freedom, it doesn't mean Paradise on Earth, because we are not forced to obey our leaders. "No rules at all" means anarchy. In anarchy, only the strong will prevail, the weak will suffer. "No rules at all" will mean Paradise on Earth for a minority that ruthlessly oppresses the majority. "No rules at all" will mean Hell on Earth for this majority.

When there are no rules at all, then the weak are not free. It may sound ridiculous, but too much freedom can really kill freedom. And this seems to be the main reason why the American Dream for all turned into an American Nightmare for many.

On the next pages, I would like to invite you to follow me on a journey to the moment, when freedom killed freedom.

The American Dream

Since its independence in the year 1776, the United States of America were the target of many dreams. The American constitution, signed in 1787, started with the famous words "We the people..." For the first time in modern history it was not a monarch who defined the rules of the state, but the people. It was less than a hundred years that the French king Louis XIV issued his famous "L'état, c'est moi" – "I am the state". What a distance had been covered by the Americans to get from the "I am the state" to "We the people"!

In Europe, the old forces were still in power at the end of the 18th century. The French revolution of the year 1789 only shook the old institutions for a short time, some years later Napoleon declared himself "Emperor" and everything was back to "normal" in Europe. Only many years later the central European countries should find their way to democracy, in Germany the first undertaking of the Weimar Republic in the 1920s ended in the terror of the nazi-regime. If you wanted to be free and no longer under the yoke of tyranny, America was the Promised Land. There you could do what you wanted. There you could be free.

But it wasn't only freedom from tyranny that the Europeans looked for in America. For many years, Europe couldn't offer a perspective for its people. You could be hard-working and yet starving. While we are now becoming too fat, our ancestors knew what hunger meant. Thousands of Irish died in the great potato famine of the 1840s. And many more died without any famine, with enough food in store – but not available to the lower classes. The upper class made sure to keep its privileges – and the lower classes simply died. Their life wasn't worth a dime.

Again this was different in America. In America, your pedigree was of no importance. If you were hard-working, you could make it. Everyone had the same chance.

Equal chances and freedom: That was the American Dream for us Europeans.

And it still is the hope for many people in developing countries, tortured by hunger, poverty and inhumane governments. They don't get any chances in their come-country, but they still believe that you can make it in America.

"From rags to riches" is the saying in America, in Germany we say "from washing dishes to being a millionaire". And if there is one country where this can become true, then it is America.

The American Dream is the hope for the forgotten and oppressed everywhere in the world. And it was more than a dream: It was real. There really was a "land of the free", the Promised Land. You just had to cross the ocean, and at the end of your journey you would find a better life. Like Noah beating the seas with his arch. America was the Paradise of our times.

The American Reality

This picture, however, is getting blurry. Today it seems that you can no longer put exclamation marks behind the statements I made about the American Dream. Especially the economical situation is getting worse. Not for the country as a whole. The economy is still growing and it is still the largest economy of the world (with China catching up – but China has four times as many people).

But for many in America, the financial situation is deteriorating. Nowadays, working hard no longer means you will make it. Working hard rather means you are lost in a poverty trap.

The growing inequality and poverty of large parts of the population is measured with the Gini coefficient. The coefficient was invented by the Italian statistician Corrado Gini, and it provides a simple way to describe how the income or the wealth is distributed within a country.

In a perfect communist society, the Gini coefficient would be 0. Everyone just owns and earns the same. Even the communist countries never reached that goal – and such a distribution of wealth would probably be considered unfair by most of us. Why should someone, who is only working one hour per day earn as much as someone who is working ten hours a day?

The other extreme would be a Gini coefficient of 1. This would be a society where nobody owns or earns anything – apart from one man who owns and earns all the money. That would be a perfect tyranny, and surely not a society you would want to live in.

So the extreme values of the Gini coefficient describe countries and economies that are in contradiction to the American Dream. A Gini coefficient that would fit to a fair society should be somewhere in between. In fact, for most of the time after the Second World War, the Gini coefficient for income distribution in America was around 0.3. The same number we can find for most European countries like France, England or Germany.

The higher the Gini coefficient the more unequal is the distribution of the income. The Brazilian economy was dominated by a handful of great land owners with the majority of the people living in great poverty for most of its time. The people didn't have access to a good education, it didn't have access to good jobs, and it didn't have the possibility to improve its life. This has only changed recently. But up to this point the Gini coefficient for Brazil was one of the highest in the world: 0.6.

History thus shows us that we don't have to reach a Gini coefficient of 1 to live in an unjust country. The rather low number of 0.6 is sufficient. A rather just distribution of income and wealth seems to be reached when the Gini coefficient is in the range of 0.3. The jackpot question now is: What is the Gini coefficient for income of the USA at the beginning of the 21st century? It is an astonishing 0.47.

If you think that might be too high, wait until you have seen the second number. The Gini coefficient for wealth in the United States has reach an all-time high of 0.8!

The income and wealth distribution is less equal in the United States than in any other industrialized country.

There are many, many people in America that are working in two, three or four jobs and still don't have enough money to make a decent living. They barely have enough money to survive.

And on the other hand you have the super-rich. Those people who buy houses for millions of dollars as easily as you would buy a new CD; those who don't only have one car but one car for each day of the year; those who don't buy their things at the next Walt-Mart around the corner, but in London or Paris.

This sounds like a typical debate out of envy. These people made it, why shouldn't they enjoy their money? Why shouldn't they live in a house with twenty bedrooms and forty bathrooms? Why shouldn't they travel around the world, buy their suits in London and their food in Paris? You could have it as well. You just have to work hard.

Well, that is the point. Can everyone have it? Can everyone have such a wealth and such a luxurious lifestyle if he only works hard enough? In this case, we could ignore the growing inequality in the USA and simply argue that this is due to a growing number of lazy people who prefer lying at the beach instead of working hard each day.

And in fact, we can read that seven out of ten billionaires in the USA made their first billion with their work, whereas in Germany most billionaires today simply inherited their wealth from their parents. So is the reason for the growing inequality in the USA simply that less people work hard – and some work harder? Can you still make it, when you really try?

If you just look at the numbers I just provided, you could have that impression. At least, most of the billionaires in America today haven't been billionaires when they were born. In Germany, on the other hand, the rich seem to stay among themselves. When you father was a billionaire, you will be a billionaire once you inherit his money. If your father was poor, the chances are low that you will be a billionaire in your lifetime. Moving from nothing to super-rich is very, very hard in Germany and in the rest of Europe.

The funny thing is: It is also very, very hard in America…

Wait a minute: We just said that seven out of ten billionaires in the USA today haven't been billionaires when they were born. So how did they make it?

The solution is simple: They made it from rich to super-rich. In most cases, the parents of today's billionaires in the USA were already millionaires. The kids inherited the money and turned the wealth in an even bigger wealth. They made it from rich to super-rich, but they never made it from nothing to super-rich.

Scientist are talking about "social mobility" when people are moving up and down the social ladder. In the feudal stated of the aristocratic Europe, the social mobility was rather low. It almost never happened that a peasant would be an aristocrat at the end of his life, as it was equally unlikely that an aristocrat would end its days as a peasant. The social classes were fixed; no-one was moving up, no-one was moving down.

That's why America was such a promise for Europeans: Social classes were virtually unknown in America. It only counted what you could do, how good you were at your job, and how hard you were willing to work. The social mobility associated with the American Dream was reaching the sky.

Even today the social mobility in Europe is rather low. You can make it from nothing to rich or super-rich, there are no legal or traditional limits any longer, but the chances are low that you will really make it. You might make it to a decent living if you start from nothing, but becoming a billionaire when you start from nothing is an exceptional case in Europe.

Everyone thinks that the social mobility in America should be factors higher than in Europe. But it is one thing what you think and another thing what you know. So some scientist set out to measure the social mobility in the old and in the new world. And they came up with a surprising result.

The data clearly showed that the social mobility in the USA, the land of the free, and the land where you can make it if you really want, is even lower than in Europe.

That finding is a severe blow to the American Dream. If you want to climb up the social ladder, don't try it in America, try it in Europe; your chances are greater here. How can this be?

Two reasons come to my mind that lead to a great inequality in the American society (and more and more in European societies): One is education, the other one is the tax system.

Education has always been regarded as a solid basis for success. The better your education as a child was, the better your income as an adult will be. Of course you have to work hard for your education. You have to learn in order to succeed. You can't expect just to go to school and by some miracle all the wisdom of the world will enter your brain without any effort. But that is okay. Why should someone succeed without effort? That wouldn't be fair.

But the willingness to learn is not everything. You also need someone to teach you. And the dividing line between education for the rich (privately financed) and education for the poor (publicly financed) is nowhere greater than in America. The rich buy themselves the best education available, while the poor get the breadcrumbs falling from the table of the rich. Their education is the worst in all civilized countries. But without the right education, you will never have the chance to succeed. The American Dream died for many Americans already when they were kids.

Even more: The rich stay among themselves from the early days on. They know each other – and they help each other. If you need a well-paid job, well, let's see if I can help you, after all, I've known you since we've met in school. Now try to enter that circle after you finished college. You'll always be a stranger to them. Officially, there is not aristocracy in America. De facto, there is. It separates the people through education.

In Europe, education is still open to everyone. But it is changing. More and more private schools are opening their gates, gathering the rich among themselves. The aristocracy is coming back to Europe, following the American example.

And once you are rich, you can be assured that your wealth will grow. Taxes are for the poor. And I am not talking about the legal and illegal tricks the rich found to circumvent the fiscal authorities. Even if a rich should pay his taxes legally, he will pay less than a poor one.

That can't be true, you would expect? After all, the tax rate is rising with your income, the more you earn, the more you pay, so the rich should pay more than the poor? That was the theory a long time ago. But nowadays, this is only true for working people, those that have a nine-to-five job or even several of them. They pay the high taxes. The rich don't make their money with hard work. They make their money with money. They invest it. And taxes for investments are ridiculously low in America. That's why the multi-millionaire and former candidate for Presidency Mitt Romney was paying a tax rate of less than 15% - although the maximum tax rate is 35% in America. The rich pay fewer taxes than their secretaries. But the secretaries need their money to live; the rich have their money to make more money. As the saying goes: "The first million is the hardest." Then it's just grabbing the money left to you by the state.

We have a similar development in Germany. The maximum tax rate is 45%, but no millionaire will ever pay it. They make their money with investments, and here the maximum tax-rate is 25%. This is still higher than in America, but it is equally unfair.

But is it really unfair? Why shouldn't the successful profit from their success? Why should the state take away their wealth and distribute it among the poor for lower taxes and better education? Isn't everyone the architect of his own future? Isn't life a struggle where only the toughest and fittest survive?

This idea is quite often identified with the work of Charles Darwin. But in fact it was Herbert Spencer who coined the phrase "Survival of the fittest". He was inspired by Darwins work, but Darwin only said that those will survive who are best adapted to their environment. These are not necessarily the fittest or strongest, after all the dinosaurs all died while little, mice-like animals – our ancestors – survived. The reason is simply that they were better adapted to a changing environment. Spencer turned "best adapted" into "fittest" and proclaimed that life is a daily struggle in which only the toughest will survive. Or as Thomas Hobbes once put it: "Homo homini lupus" – "Man is a wolf to his fellow man". Humans are involved in an endless fight against each other.

And life really seems to be a daily struggle and fight in America. As a tourist in America, you often get the warning not to visit certain quarters of the city. And if you are in these quarters, don't stop at red lights, because you might be attacked in the few seconds that you are waiting for the light to turn green.

In fact, there is no civilized country with more killings per capita than the United States. While there are more than 500 people killed in cities like Chicago, Washington, and Los Angeles per year (in each of the cities!), there are only 800 people killed in the whole of Germany – with a population of 82 million!

Some years ago we had the case of a "cannibal" in Germany. It was s gruesome story of a man who had killed another one and had eaten part of his flesh. This story even made it into American newspapers and I remember reading a description of the crime in the USA while I was there. But what I remember most about the article was a little comment of the journalist. After having described the horrible crime he felt the necessity to add that, in spite of all the brutality in this case, Germany is a much safer place to live than America.

It was during one of my first visits to America that I made contact with the general violence and fear of violence that seem to be daily business for Americans. I was living in a small hotel in a suburb of a mid-sized city. Our company had a small production facility nearby; it was what I would call a typical middle-class region in a southern state of the USA.

I had just arrived after more than eight hours in the plane. The weather was great, the sun was still up in the sky, and the air was warm. I felt a little bit hungry and knew that there was a supermarket some few hundred meters away. Taking profit of the nice weather, I walked there, bought some things and walked back to the hotel. I would never have thought that this could be a big deal. I changed my mind, when I mentioned this the next morning to my American colleagues. They couldn't believe that I had taken the risk of walking unprotected, without any shelter e.g. from a car. They made clear that I shouldn't do this again; it simply was much too dangerous.

Needless to say I followed their advice. But I never felt the inclination to give an American visitor in Germany the same advice. Even I walk to supermarkets in Germany without feeling threatened. But then: The crime rate in Germany is much lower than in the US.

I thought that someone had made a mistake when I first read about the number of prisoners in the USA. Can you believe that roughly one percent of the American population is behind bars in this moment? Now I understand why you are expecting a crime around every corner in the USA. The number of prisoners is ten times higher in the USA than it is in Europe. In Germany, the exact percentage of people behind bars is 0.08%. And it isn't so low because we can't afford to build more prisons or the criminals are not found by the police. It is just that the crime rates are much lower.

The struggle for life, the daily fight seems to be much more of a reality in the USA than in Europe. America is a much more violent society than Europe.

One fact that supports this statement is the simple fact that America still has the death penalty. I don't want to discuss the fact that mainly colored people are sentenced to death ("…only one color dead", as Peter Gabriel once sang, although the song was about the apartheid in South Africa), that many death sentences were simply wrong, and that many innocent get killed by the society. Leave that apart. I only want to discuss what using the death penalty tells us about a society.

There was a time when the death penalty was common practice in every country. In Germany it was abolished after the horrors of the nazi-regime, in France it was only abolished in 1981, although rarely used the years before. In older times, however, the death penalty was regularly applied – and very popular. History tells us about the remarkable imagination that humans showed when devising now methods how to kill a man. Crucifixion is known from the Bible, but people were also quartered, cooked in oil or burnt on the stake. The Romans invited the people to watch criminals being devoured by wild animals in their arenas. History tells us that these kinds of killing were very popular among the people.

Nowadays, these public massacres wouldn't be possible anymore. Our society is much less violent than it used to be. So it declared any cruel punishment to be illegal (that is even part of the American constitution), and many countries abolished death penalty as the cruelest punishment. For the punishment you apply to your criminals is less a sign of the crime they committed; it is only a sign of cruelty and violence of the society. The more violent the society the more cruel is the punishment. That's why America still has the death penalty. It is the most violent society in the Western world.

America is at war. But it is not the war against terrorists; it is a war against itself.

In the civil war, the dividing line in America has been between the north and the south, those that wanted to abolish slavery, and those that wanted to keep it. Nowadays, the dividing line cannot be drawn on a map any longer. It is a dividing line in every village, in every city, in every state. It is a dividing line that goes straight through the American people. It is a dividing line that separates the rich from the poor.

You can make it, if you really want. I guess that is one of the fundamental doctrines of the American spirit. But what happens, if you don't get the chance? If you struggle and run, but you are only running in a hamster wheel without getting any further? Do you think you're being treated fair?

You would probably look for other ways to improve your situation. And if there is no way within the rules of the society, you will break them. With the aristocracy of the wealthy keeping the people down and away from their places, the only way to improve your lot is by using violence. Thus the much higher crime rate in the USA compared to Europe.

The Romans were using "bread and circuses" to keep the people entertained, to let them forget that they were without any rights. But they had one power. At the end of a fight between gladiators, when one was lying in the sand, the other one standing above him, victoriously, they could decide about the fate of the looser. Thumb down meant death, thumb up meant he could live for the moment.

The people were deciding about life and death of a human being. What greater power can there be? And in today's America the death penalty is declared "in the name of the people". To let them feel powerful, although they don't have anything to say? To let them believe in the American Dream where everyone can make it, even become so powerful as to decide about the life and death of another man?

These thoughts are hopefully too cynical to be true. So let's finish this small chapter with the observation that the social mobility in America today is lower than in Europe. That getting from "rags to riches" is only a myth and no longer reality, because the rich keep themselves and their wealth among themselves. The American people don't simply accept it, but they resort to violence to get their share of the wealth of the society, as there is no way to improve their situation within in the rules of the society. And this makes America the most violent country in the Western world.

One part of the American Dream, the dream that you can make it, is only a dream nowadays. But what about the second part, what about freedom? Isn't America still he freest country in the world? The country where everybody can speak his mind, the country where everybody can do what he likes and no dictator is limiting his freedom?

It probably is. But it is probably this unlimited freedom in America which is the root cause for its problems – and the disappearance of the American Dream.

The Fight for Freedom

Can there be too much freedom? It sounds unbelievable. When we look back in history, there was never the question of too much freedom, only of too less. In Europe, we don't have to go back that much in time to find a time when freedom was definitely lacking. It was lacking for the communist countries up to the end of the 1980s, it was lacking for Germany and many parts of Europe until the end of the Second World War.

Only when freedom was established, when the people had the right to mind their own business, when a free press was established that had a close look at what the powerful where doing, and when everyone had the chance to get a better life if he only was willing to work hard, only when this was established, life became better for everyone. People lead a better life today than they did thirty years ago under communist rule. When the nazi-regime was defeated, the German economy started its legendary growth which is sometimes called "the economic miracle". Leading a better life and limitless freedom seem to go hand in hand.

On the other hand: Whenever there was a lack of freedom, there was great poverty among the people. The truth of this statement can be traced back to the first sign of human civilization in Mesopotamia. Only a small minority could lead a life in luxury and freedom, the majority was leading a life not much better than the cattle, hardly having enough to survive, clad in rags, eating rotten food if any food was available at all, working the whole day with no time for recreation or even vacation.

Human civilization advanced, but the general social structure didn't change. Thousands of people worked hard to build the pyramids in Egypt – but their life was a life of poverty and deprivation. And they didn't have the possibility to improve it. Education and medical care were only accessible to the upper class, the aristocrats. They stayed among themselves, a peasant never had the chance to climb the social ladder and become a pharaoh one day.

The Roman Empire conquered the world, but the social structure remained. In the 5th century before Christ the poor had left the city and gone on strike to ask for better working and living conditions. The upper class had sent the consul Menenius Agrippa to talk to them. And he told them a story: There once had been a time when all limbs of the body had their own will and their own language. And the limbs grew tired of the fact that all their hard work only served the stomach that was lazily lying around. So they decided to go on strike: The hands didn't bring any more food to the mouth, the mouth didn't accept any food and the teeth no longer chewed it. Hunger, they thought, would be their weapon to defeat the stomach. But not much time passed, and the whole body weakened. At this point they understood that the stomach is not idle and useless. Just as he was fed by the limbs, he was supporting the limbs in his way. Only together, stomach and limbs, they would succeed in keeping the whole body alive.

Thus the limbs stopped their strike and went back to work. So did the peasant, as the legend goes, after they had heard Agrippa's story.

The Christian Middle Ages had a similar story to keep the poor at its place. This time, of course, it was taken from the Bible. It is a story about Noah. Once Noah had drunken too much wine, and his son Ham had made fun of his drunken father. As revenge, Noah had cursed Ham and his entire descendants to be servant to all other man. The peasants of the Middle Ages, so the general understanding, were descendants of Ham – and it was thus their destination to serve the nobles.

And neither in Roman times, nor in the Middle Ages there was a chance for the poor to lead a better life one day. There life was destined, they would not be able to change it, nor would their descendants. They just had to follow the orders of the upper class like a flock of sheep.

The concentration of power in the hands of just a few men reached its climax in the 17th and 18th century in Europe. This time is also known as the time of absolutism, when monarchs throughout Europe concentrated all the power in the land in their hands. It was the time when Louis XIV made his famous statement "L'état, c'est moi" (I am the state).

And it was the time, when more and more people fled from Europe and looked for a better life in America.

The majority of peasants were used to such a treatment. They had never known another life and they were told that they could never expect another life. But this time the absolute monarch had gone too far. In their desire to control every aspect of the life of their citizens that had taken everything in their hands: The army, the police, the courts, the finances, and even the economy, using an economic system called mercantilism. The upper class became less and less powerful – and they were not used to it.

The counts and barons always had a certain liberty in their doings. They were the kings on their own land and not used to giving power to an absolute ruler.

For the first time in history there was something like a rebellion against the rulers. Not from the very poor who had all the reason to rebel, but from the upper class that saw its privileges fading away.

Already in the middle of the 17th century, the English upper class rebelled against the absolute monarch King Karl. This resulted in the English civil war that lasted from 1642 to 1649. In the end, the king was captured and decapitated – and the upper class got back its rights. The model kingdom of our times lived without a king for forty years, until they invited Wilhelm III to become the new king – if he signed the "Bill of Rights" that ensured certain rights to the people (meaning the upper class). He did it, and the English had a king up to this time.

The story was different in France. Here the upper class also rebelled against the intention of the king to concentrate all the power of the state in his own hands and to downgrade the nobles to nothing more than well-clothed slaves. But King Louis XIV was astute. He didn't fight his opponents – he invited them to his new built castle in Versailles and made them experience every luxury he could think of. After some time, the aristocrats got used to this sumptuous lifestyle and even addicted to it. They spend large amounts of money to keep up with the king, and in many cases they even spent more money than they actually had. But the king was more than willing to help them out and lend them some money. And then he had them in his hands. They had to stay in Versailles because all important decisions were made there, but they only could stay in Versailles as long as they had the king's favor because they owed him money. Getting his favor thus became the prominent occupation of the French nobles, eliminating any thought of rebellion against him. The nobles were trapped in a golden cage.

The time of absolutism was the time when liberal philosophers demanded more rights for the people. In the beginning, this only included the upper class, just like the Greek democracy was only a democracy for the male rich – the rest of the population, the females and the poor had no rights whatsoever.

But the upper class was changing in these times. Merchants became active in the trade between Europe and the new colonies in Africa, Asia and the Americas. Just by selling goods they collected a fortune that was comparable to the wealth of the old aristocracy. Some, like the Fugger-family in Augsburg, Germany, became so rich that they even helped kings to finance their wars (of course in exchange to certain trade privileges that made them even richer).

This new upper class also claimed their rights, and they got it. Democracy improved step by step in Europe. While America already promised freedom for every citizen, this dream was only slowly realized in Europe.

Up to the beginning of the 20th century, Germany had a three-class franchise. The whole population (the population that could vote, i.e. all male adults) was divided into three groups depending on their tax payments. In each group, the men paid one third of the direct taxes. The first group started with the wealthiest tax payer and went down until one third of total tax revenues were reached. The second group started with the first one paying less taxes than the last one of the first group and went on down until the second third of taxes was reached. The last group was for the poorest tax payers.

The result was that almost all voters were collected in the last group, but this one had only one third of the votes. The first two groups, just a handful of men, quite often only one man in each group, had two thirds of the votes. So in the end, the rich decided about the politics in Germany.

This rule was abolished in 1918, when the German Emperor Wilhelm II was forced to resign and the first true democratic state in Germany was founded. Since that time, the rule "one man, one vote" applies in Germany, and finally, after thousands of years of deprivation, even the poor have some power in our society.

The first steps into democracy found a severe rupture when Hitler took power, but after the atrocities of the Second World War a stable democracy was finally established in Germany. Roughly two hundred years after it was done in America.

And it was since then that life got definitely better in Germany. And it is not a coincidence that freedom and an improved life-quality come in pairs. You cannot improve the life of the people without freedom. You can improve the life of some of the people without freedom. The aristocracies that ruled the world for centuries proved it; the dictatorships all over the world prove it. It is very easy for a minority in a country to become richer without true freedom in their country. But it is impossible to improve the lives of all without freedom.

There might be several reasons for this. But one reason definitely is that you cannot improve your lifestyle and technology without freedom. Technological advances that made the industrial revolution possible, that are changing our world on an almost daily scale and are thus providing well-paid jobs to many people, would not be possible without freedom. If you don't have the freedom to publish unusual thoughts, to make statements that contradict what seems to be the well-known truth, there would be no change.

Einstein's theory of relativity looks completely strange, as does the theory of quantum mechanics. Their statements contradict common sense all the time, for instance the statement that time passes slower when you reach the speed of light. But they are correct, you can measure the predictions of these strange theories, and they have proved correct.

It needs freedom to change if a society wants to improve ecologically, economically or socially. But dictators fear changes. A dictator will always try to protect his position, which means he has to prevent any changes, because one of those changes might affect his position, and might push him from his throne.

It is no coincidence that nazi-scientist invented an "Aryan" science that tried to explain the world without using the theory of relativity or the quantum theory which was considered to be "Jewish". When it's strange, kill it – or it will kill you. Competition is not wanted in an unfree society, whereas it is the very basis of a democratic society. So you do everything to keep competition away.

One example for this can again be found in German history. The Ruhr valley in the north of Cologne was a forgotten valley until the 18th century. Then someone found coal in the valley, the gold of the industrial revolution. This changed the look of this region completed: Starting with some villages, the region is now one of the most densely populated regions in Europe, with a population of roughly ten million. Since the end of the 19th century, the Ruhr valley was one of the economical centers of Germany. It was comparable to London and Paris in its size and economical power (though not its cultural or political importance). Yet it was only in the 1960s when the first university opened its gates in the valley.

The reason was not that politics had no intention to do this. But the powerful coal barons, the economical lords of the valley, opposed any plan to open a university in the valley. They feared that with a good education, the workers would no longer bear their miserable lot and might claim more rights – and this was something the upper class always tried to keep away from the poor.

Only when the coal industry became less important and the power of the coal barons dwindled, the politicians could open universities in the valley. There are half a dozen of them right now, including the largest university in Germany.

A better life and freedom for all go hand in hand. When only the upper class has the freedom to do as it wants, only they will have a decent living while the lower class lives in poverty. As long as the upper class tries to protect its position and keeps freedom away for the masses, there is no chance that they will have a better living. Only when there is freedom for all, when everybody can participate in the society, everyone will be better off.

But that, you would say, is exactly the situation in the "land of the free". So where is the problem?

When Freedom Kills Freedom

I you were asked to define freedom, what would be your answer? You would probably say something like: I have freedom when I can do whatever I want; when there is nobody who comes in my way and hinders me from doing as I please.

With this definition you would probably describe the very essence of "freedom". If you could do whatever you like, you would be ultimately free. But then: You are not the only person in the world. There are others who live in the same country, the same city, the same household with you. Would such a definition of freedom be a practical rule if we try to live with others? Do we really accept that the other can do as he pleases when we try to live with him?

Imagine someone who just throws his garbage on the street as he doesn't like to walk to the garbage can. Should he be allowed to do this? Imagine someone who simply doesn't accept personal property and takes whatever he likes – jewels, cars, money, or just a sandwich – from others. Should he be allowed to do this?

You probably agree with me that such a behavior shouldn't be allowed. So the definition of freedom as "Everyone can do as he likes" is not a practical definition. It wouldn't work if you try to live with others. In a community of people, the rule of freedom should be something like: "Everyone can do as he likes – unless he doesn't limit the freedom of others with his actions."

So when I throw my garbage on the street, I ask others to clean the street – or to live with the rats that will inevitably show up. This is definitely limiting the freedom of others, as they are forced to behave in a way they wouldn't like. Simply taking the possession of others would limit their freedom to handle their property as they want. This would also limit their freedom to act. These behaviors are therefore not compatible with a just definition of freedom.

The rule pronounced as "Do not unto others as you would have others do unto you" is actually known as the Golden Rule of Morality. It is mention in the Bible (Matthew 7) as:

"So in everything, do to others what you would have them do to you."

And the German philosopher Immanuel Kant phrased it at the end of the 18th century in his famous categorical imperative: "Act only according to that maxim whereby you can, at the same time, will that it should become a universal law."

Kant's version sounds much more elaborate than the Golden Rule, but it basically means the same. And he explicitly mentioned in his "Critique of Practical Reason" that he didn't intend to define a new moral law, because he didn't assume that mankind had lived without a moral law before his writings. In fact, he only wanted to show that this Golden Rule is our inborn moral law. Every man has it from the day he is born (unless he has some severe psychological problems). It is the basic law that guides human morality.

When we try to define freedom, we cannot only take into account our own personal wishes, but we have to make sure that we do not restrict the freedom of others. We have to act as if our acting could become a universal law. This means that we have to restrict our freedom. Limitless freedom wouldn't work in a society as we would continuously limit the freedom of others. We can only have true freedom when we have rules.

The result seems contradictory. But a valid definition of freedom requires that we limit our freedom. We need rules that limit our freedom so everyone can experience the maximum freedom.

If we had no rules at all, if everyone could do as he pleases, then we wouldn't have freedom. It sounds like the ultimate and perfect freedom, but in fact its anarchy. If everyone can do as he wants, the strong and the ruthless will define the rules in the end. Limitless freedom, ironically, will bring us back to the times when a small aristocracy ruled the world. The aristocracy justified its power by divine ancestry – and kept it up by violence. The new aristocracy got its power by violence. But maybe someday they will justify it also by some higher means. If this isn't divine ancestry, maybe its physical superiority – they simply were better and worked harder than everyone else.

Anarchy, a society without rules, might look like the perfect free society. But in fact it is the death of any free society. And though it sounds promising at first glance, no-one wants to live in such a society.

This was shown in a nice experiment that came in the disguise of a little game. The test persons got a certain amount of money. They could invest the money in a project. When everyone had put the amount of money he wanted to invest into a central bank, a certain interest was added to the amount and then the whole money was distributed among the players equally. I.e. someone who invested much more than the average even lost money in this round, someone who didn't invest at all, only made money.

The players were separated into two groups. There were absolutely no behavioral rules in the first group, while the second group had the possibility to define rules, e.g. to punish someone when the majority thought he wouldn't play fair. After each round, the players could decide if they wanted to stay in their group or move to the other group.

In the beginning, almost every test person joined the first group. After all, playing without rules seems to be the perfect world. But already in the first rounds some players didn't invest any money, they just cashed in. The second group started to punish players that acted this way, while the players of the first group simply had to accept such a behavior, after all, they didn't have any rules in their group.

But they didn't accept it for long: After only a few rounds of the game, almost everyone had joined the second group, where at this time no more punishments had to be pronounced as everyone behaved morally.

A completely free society is a society no-one really would like to live in. It only helps the strong and the ruthless, while it punishes the poor and morally acting people. The strong have all the freedom, the poor lose theirs. A completely free society is a society where freedom kills freedom.

It might sound contradictory, but we need rules to have freedom for all and not just for the strong and the ruthless. This brings up two questions: What should the rules look like – and who should watch over them?

Rules for Freedom

The Golden Rule is the basic rule of human morality. But it is a rather general rule; it is a basic rule like the constitution of a country. How do we come from such a basic rule to some more detailed rules and laws that guide our lives?

We could think of many rules, and everybody would probably find arguments why his rules would be in accordance with the Golden Rule – even if his rules contradicts another proposed rule that also claims to be in full accordance with the Golden Rule. How do we decide which rule is the right one, which rule is just?

Kant gave us a hint: He demanded that a proposed rule (or an action) should be a universal law. This simple request has a huge implication: It demands that all people are treated equally before the law. No group can request a certain set off rules, as the aristocrats had their set of rules and the peasants another one. "All men are created equal" as it says in the declaration of independence of the United States. This, in fact, is the basic rule of all democratic societies. Not to be treated as a person of second class anymore but to have the same rights as everybody else was the main reason why so many people left Europe and moved to America in the 18th and 19th century, and why people from all over the world are still doing it today.

The same set of rules applies to everyone; no-one is above the law. That is the first request to a just set of rules. And it is the reason why the Lady Justice is blindfolded.

This, however, still doesn't describe how we can find a just set of rules that assure that everybody is treated justly and which assure that there is not one group that will profit from the rules while the majority suffers under them.

The American philosopher John Rawls provided an answer to that question in the second half of the 20th century. He described a thought experiment. Let us assume, he said, that we are living in a society without any moral rules, so that we are able to define our own rules right from the start, and this time make it right. In order to define the rules, everybody sits together and makes proposals. The group then decides in a democratic vote (one man, one vote) which proposal should then become a rule for the whole community.

That sounds like a smart approach. At least it is a democratic approach, so it looks basically right. There is only one problem with it: We don't just have people sitting together and defining the rules for the community. We have poor people and rich people sitting together; homeless people and owners of large villas; men and women; black and white; landowners and peons; investors and savers. Everyone has a certain history, has a certain background, and has certain interests. When these people sit together, there is a risk that they do not define rules that could be universal laws, but only rules that would make life easier for their specific group. Unjust proposals could fail the voting, but there is a risk that they could make it as not everyone understands all implications of a proposed rule and thus assumes that a friendly looking rule will remain friendly – and not one day turn against oneself.

Rawls understood that his thought experiment was incomplete. Just have everybody sitting together would not guarantee that just and moral laws would be generated. So he added another feature to his experiment: The veil of ignorance.

Rawls assumed that we can only come up with just rules if we don't know our position in the society. Only if we don't know if we are rich or poor, if we are an employer or an employee, or if we are homeless or own several houses will we be able to propose just rules.

We have to make these decisions under the "veil of ignorance". Only in this case we will not try to propose laws that will improve the situation for a certain group, because we cannot be sure to belong to this group – or to the group that will suffer under this unjust rule.

Even though Rawls was a philosopher and thus probably had to live with the prejudice that philosophers are living in their ivory towers with no connection to reality, he knew that his thought experiment would always be just that, a thought experiment, and that there would never be the possibility to turn it into reality. After all, we already have a set of rules – as just or unjust they might be. And we know ourselves; we know the group we belong to.

Rawls saw his procedure to define just rules as an ideal procedure. He knew that it was not a template for our acting. But he wanted to describe the ideal procedure to challenge us to find a procedure that would bring us as close as possible to this ideal world.

Rawls wanted everyone to understand that we cannot define laws from which only a small minority will profit. We cannot have laws that only consider the special interest of a certain group, but we need laws that are in the interest of the majority. He thus proposed that the laws and their consequences should be openly discussed before they were voted in Parliament. This would allow everyone to understand the consequences of the laws on the different groups in the society. And it would make clear to everyone if the law was in the interest of all (or the majority) or if it was just in the interest of a small elite. He hoped that public pressure would make it difficult to vote laws that are only in the interest of a minority – and against the interest of the majority.

Because this is the main claim for just laws: The rules should apply to everyone and be in the interest of the majority. If they were only in the interest of a minority, then they wouldn't be just – and they wouldn't be democratic. In this case we would have the same situation as during the feudal times in Europe, when the aristocrats had their personal set of rules that helped them to keep their power and oppress the majority.

So if we think that it is just that richer people should pay higher taxes then we shouldn't come up with rules that regard income from speculation – the main source of income for the rich – as another kind of income where lower taxes apply. This is a rule only a minority profits from – and it is therefore definitely not a just rule.

When we define rules, we need to make sure that they are in the interest of the majority and not only in the interest of a small but powerful minority. These rules would be unjust – and could never become a universal law.

The Protector of Freedom

Freedom is not, as many might assume, a "laissez-faire", a "do what you want". It is a maximum freedom within certain boundaries given by our inborn moral sentiment and written down by the society.

However, not everyone seems to have a "moral compass", an inborn moral sentiment that lets him act according to the Golden Rule of Morality. On the contrary, some ruthless people don't give a damn about how others might suffer from their doings, and sadistic people even might enjoy that others are suffering. We can't just rely on nature to ensure that everyone will act in a moral way and that someone will not kill freedom by requesting too much freedom for himself.

So someone has to make sure that the rules are followed. Someone needs to be the caretaker of freedom.

In a democratic state, there is only one answer to that: This someone has to be us. We have to watch over the rules and make sure they are being followed; we have to make sure that no-one gathers so much power that he kills the freedom of other people.

The problem is only: There are so many of us. How shall we look after each other?

It was easy when a community just consisted of a few dozen people. They could take make sure that no-one acted selfishly and harmed others with his doings. It was the time of the Middle Ages, when the peasants of a village owned their fields and meadows collectively. The whole community decided who could bring how many cattle onto the meadows, so the meadows wouldn't be stressed by too many animals in one year and grow less grass in the next year. They made sure that no-one acted selfishly, brought too many animals on the meadows, earned a lot of money and next year the whole village suffered from his selfish act. Commons like these lasted for centuries in England, and can even be found in some remote valleys in the Alps today.

But when the size of the community increases, when you have to look after too many people, you are unable to cope with it. And society with thousands or millions of people cannot work in the same way a small village works.

That's why civilization invented the state. In the first millennia, the state was practically owned by the aristocrats who used it and its people to support their luxury lifestyle. Nowadays, at least in the Western world, we live in a democratic society. Our rulers are rulers for a certain time; they have an "expiration date". If we don't like what they do, we simply don't re-elect them.

Our politicians represent the people. We live in a representative democracy. The politicians might do a bad job, but then it is for us to stop them and change it. That's what democracy is all about.

We elect a government and we empower the government to make sure, that the rules are followed. It uses the bureaucrats and the police to reach this goal, but in the end they do it because we want them to do it.

The protector of freedom, therefore, is the state.

*

You might imagine that we have some prejudices about Americans in Europe. Nothing serious, and believe me, there are also prejudices against the French in Germany as there are against the German in France. Some are probably less a prejudice than only a stereotype, just as a Frenchman is always supposed to be running around with his baguette.

One of these stereotypes is the reaction that I would expect from Americans when they read: "The protector of freedom is the state". I would imagine that most Americans start to wonder if I have lost my mind. The state, as we understand the American point-of-view, is the enemy. He represents the opposite of freedom. The stronger the state is, the weaker is freedom. A strong state is synonymous to communism. Just look at the former communist countries where you had a strong state! Just look at the feudal states in Europe of the 16th and 17th century where the people had no freedom and the state, the aristocracy held all the power in its hand! How can the state be the protector of freedom!

Well, not any state. Only the democratic state is the protector of freedom. The difference is that a democratic state defines the general rules and makes sure they are not broken. The communist or the absolute monarchy dictates every action. This state does not only define some boundary condition for the economy, but it defines in detail what should be produced and when.

Such a state is the enemy of freedom. But the state that claims "we the people"; the state which is ruled by the people and for the people, this state is the protector of freedom.

Communism as a synonym for complete loss of freedom and anarchy as a synonym for complete freedom are not antagonists. They only seem to be. In the end you come up with a small elite that rules the country and a majority that is oppressed by this elite. In the end, there is no difference between communism and complete freedom – as unbelievable as it may sound in first place. Both will lead to a society where the majority of the people lose their freedom and only a small minority, the strong and the ruthless who don't give a damn about moral laws, prevail.

Whit this in mind, you wonder why the Americans see the state and the government as its enemy.

The Assault on the State

There is certainly one truth in the American behavior: Don't trust the powerful. Even if they were elected in a democratic election, they will have a tendency to abuse the power that was given to them. That is why we don't just have a government and hope they will do the right thing for the time of their mandate, but we have a Parliament that has to agree to the decisions of the government and thus has to ensure that they represent the will of the people. That's why we have divided the powers in the state in legislation, jurisdiction and executive. This ensures that people don't get too much power in their hands. That's why we have a Supreme Court that watches over the laws and assures that they don't breach the constitution. That's why we have a free press that unrelentingly watches over what the powerful are doing.

In the course of time, mankind has developed many safety systems to ensure that the powerful don't abuse their power – because power corrupts – or that, if they do, they will be punished for their wrong-doings.

The democratic system might not be perfect, but it is the best to keep the powerful from oppressing the weak. Or as the former British Prime-Minister Winston Churchill once put it: "Democracy is the worst form of government, except for all those other forms that have been tried from time to time."

However, every powerful man can abuse its power. How come that the Americans only mistrust the politicians, but not great landowners or managers of multinational companies whose yearly revenue sometimes is even bigger than that of small nations? Washington as the seat of the government seems to be a synonym for corruption and selfishness and untrustworthiness. No one else in the USA seems to have such a bad press than the government and the state. Some managers, however, are definitely more powerful than most of the politicians working in Washington. But they don't get the blame.

So it seems that the Americans don't mistrust the powerful. They just don't trust the state.

This is probably due to the origin of most Americans. They fled from feudal, dictatorial and authoritarian countries where the state was limiting the freedom of its people in an unacceptable way. But today's Americans fled to America because America is a democracy, because America is different. In a democracy, the people have the possibility to punish the rulers if they misbehave. In a dictatorship, the people are afraid of its rulers. In a democracy, the rulers are afraid of the people.

Nevertheless, the Americans seem to think that they would be better off without a government and without the state, even though they have a well-established democracy and many means to control their government. There are not many countries where the people are so powerful.

But the state is the enemy. More power for the state is communism. You can hear this from almost every politician, in almost every show. It is common knowledge in America. But even if it is common knowledge now, someone must have invented it in the first place.

Of course, with their history of escaping from dictatorships, the Americans easily accepted the statement that the state is bad. But who brought up this statement?

It is probably difficult to find the originator of it, if there even is one. But maybe it helps to look at who profits from it?

I described that the state is needed as the protector of freedom. If the state were eliminated – who could replace it? There seems to be the opinion that each man can make sure for himself that he is treated justly. After all, every man in the USA has a weapon (or is at least allowed to carry a gun). So he can defend himself against unjust behavior of his aggressors. Like Gary Cooper in the movie "High noon" in his solitary fight against Frank Miller and his gang. One man against the world – and he will succeed.

But is this a realistic picture? In reality, you wouldn't stand a chance against a ruthless enemy. There is no A-Team that you can contact and that will help you against criminals who think they can take the law in their own hands and rule according to the statement of Louis XIV: "I am the state".

Only if the aggressor fears he might lose, you have a chance to stand up to him. But for this, you need an army; you need a big coalition that supports you. And there is no bigger coalition than the whole society, represented by the state. Without the state and its police or institutions to help you, you wouldn't stand a chance. You would lose your freedom or even more. With the state, you have a chance to keep your freedom.

Without a state, only those rich and powerful enough to form their own army and coalition will prevail. Without a state we have anarchy, where only a small minority wins and the majority loses.

Thus, a weak state is only in the interest of the rich and powerful. Without a state they can define their own laws and enforce them. They have all the freedom they can dream of.

The poor and weak, the small people who try to live a moral live, will lose without the state. Their freedom will be restricted by the new elite that only plays to its rules.

A weak state is only in the interest of the rich and powerful. They will profit from a world without a state. So if someone came up with the statement that life would be better without a state, it must have been someone from the upper class. And it is a lie.

Consider the irony: The absolute monarchs in Europe had made it clear that all the power is in their hands and that no-one in their countries had any rights and that no-one was free.

In today's America, everybody is told that he lives in a free country and in "the land of the free". But in fact the American search for freedom is killing the freedom for everyone apart from a small elite. America talks about freedom and is moving towards anarchy where a rich and powerful minority has taken over the power in the country. In the name of freedom, the government decides laws that allow the rich to reduce their taxes well below the tax level of the workers, and it decides laws that allow the elite to reduce their responsibility towards the community.

The poor are left to themselves. Without money, they don't have the freedom to decide how they would like to live or how their illness should be treated. They only have the freedom to suffer and die – which they do even more frequently. The average life expectancy of a rich American today is twenty years higher than the average life expectancy of a poor American.

There is not much freedom left for the lower end of society.

It is only in the interest of the rich that the myth is kept alive that the state is the enemy. So they don't have to follow any rules and can do as they want. The majority suffers. They need the state as the protector of freedom.

Capitalism vs. Market Economy

The social interactions of human beings in a state are interactions on many levels. They can be neighbors, they can have the same hobby, they can work together, they can live together, or they can do business with each other. This last interaction is in fact the dominating interaction of our today's life. Our economy defines how and where we work, which hobby we can afford to have, where we live, and what our private life looks like.

The communists showed us how an economy shouldn't look like. The standard of living of communist societies was well below the standard of living we got used to in the Western world. And, ironically, the environmental damage the communist economy inflicted was even greater than the damage in the West. Because in the West we have a free society, and the people made the clear statement that they wouldn't tolerate an unlimited damaging of the environment any longer. So institutions like the EPA were founded in US and in other Western countries, and the industry had to adapt their products and production processes to new, environmental-friendly rules.

Our economic system seems to be the perfect fit to the democratic, political system. We have freedom in our economy as we have freedom in politics.

The economical system is called capitalism or market economy. Sometimes you can also here the expression "free enterprise" instead of "market economy". But in fact these three words don't mean the same. There is a huge difference between capitalism and market economy, as there also is a difference between anarchy (which will turn into dictatorship) and democracy.

We can understand the difference if we take a closer look at how markets work. The market is a place where people buy and sell things. The price of a product is defined by the market forces, i.e. the play between demand and supply. If too many products are offered on the market, the price will go down until equilibrium is reached where supply and demand have reached the same level. On the other hand, if the demand is higher than the supply, the price will rise until the demand has decreased to the level of the available supply. No-one can simply define the price. If there were such a person, the market would collapse. The communist economy was an economy where the price was defined by the state and not by the market forces – and everybody knows the consequences.

But it is also possible that the market can collapse in our economy. This is the case when we have a monopoly acting on a market. Without competition, the monopoly can simply define the price for its products and doesn't have to care about the price that would be found if the market forces were in force.

A monopoly behaves in an economy as a dictator does in politics. If a market shall exist, it needs freedom to balance demand and supply and find the right price for a certain good. This means, that market players have to follow certain rules. None of them, for instance, can be allowed to become so powerful that he can dictate the price of a product. In this case, he would act like a monopoly and the market would cease to exist.

Thus, the market economy is the perfect match for a democracy. Both need freedom from a powerful ruler to exist – but both can only exist if they have rules that limit the freedom and ensure that no-one can become so powerful that he can overthrow democracy or the market and replace it by his authoritarian, i.e. dictatorial or monopolistic structures.

Now, where does capitalism fit into this picture?

A capitalist is a man who invests money in a business to make more money. He has a very single-minded approach to economy. And he has only one goal: Maximize the profits.

A capitalist doesn't really care what he is producing. He might not even be producing anything, as today many capitalists just speculate on the stock market to make money with money, simply omitting the painful process of producing some goods in-between. All he cares about is: How can I maximize my profits?

There is one simply solution to that question: Get rid of all competition. Without competition, you can define the prices and thus maximize your profits. So what capitalists are looking for isn't a market economy, instead he prefers a monopoly to maximize his profits, or just any kind of legislation that will help him to sell his products more easily than his competition. Anything helps that allows him to define the price of his product, anything helps that gets rid of the market.

Capitalism is the perfect match for a dictatorship. That's why capitalism also worked in Chile under Pinochet or in today's China. Capitalism doesn't require a democracy, far from it. A market economy does.

We don't see this difference when we talk about our economical system. Capitalism or market economy: That is all the same for us. And the English usage of the word "free enterprise" for "market economy" helps to increase the confusion. Free enterprise shall mean the same as market economy, but in fact it puts a focus on the freedom of the enterprises. Let them be free and do whatever they want, and the economy will prosper. But there is more to a market than only the enterprises. There is more to a market than just the supply. You also need the demand or the economy will collapse. Both of them need to be free or a market won't work. If you only assure that one side of them gets unlimited freedom, this will lead to slavery for the other side.

We have the same situation as in a society: Unlimited freedom in a society leads to anarchy with the strong and ruthless possessing all the freedom – and the weak and morally living losing their freedom.

And if you only assure freedom for enterprises in your economy, the customers, the people, will suffer. The market will cease to exist. That's why capitalism and market economy are not identical – but deadly enemies.

Quite often we can hear that managers and politicians complain that certain legislations will damage the market. But do they really mean the market – or just the selfish requirements of the companies? It is worth to take a closer look at the proposed legislation: Does it really damage the market (then it would be bad) or only capitalism (then there is a great chance that it would be great).

One example is the privatization of public companies. This has been done extensively in America with the UK following closely. But privatization is also a hobby of politicians in continental Europe.

The idea seems to be great: Business like power supplies or water supplies are brought to the market and everybody knows that markets are a good thing. Real professionals are taking over the business; the public companies no longer have to suffer under the incompetency of bureaucrats. The companies will flourish under the market rules.

This might be the case, although there are numerous examples that privatized companies only flourished for some time because the private owner reduced the wages of the employees and reduced the periodic maintenance costs. But that should not be part of our discussion.

We better take a look at the statement, that by privatizing a public company, we bring it to the market. Is this really the case?

A market needs competition; a market will cease to exist if one company can define the price as this is the case for a monopoly. Public companies have quite often been public monopolies. So by selling them to a private investor, we only exchange a public monopoly by a private monopoly. By selling the business, the state created capitalism – and stroke a deadly blow to the market.

A market only works if no company gets strong enough to define the rules of the business. If this is the case the market dies and is replaced by some anarchic dictatorship.

A wonderful example is the financial sector. Dozens of banks around the world have been declared to be "too-big-to-fail". So whatever they do, how much money they might lose with their speculations – they have a state guarantee that they will survive. The general rule that you have to go bankrupt if you lose too much money no longer applies to them.

But if a market player positions himself outside the general market rules, he becomes a danger to the market economy and to our democracy. Such a player will define the rules of the game like a dictator. We simply cannot accept this, if we want to keep our freedom and don't want to become slaves to the banks.

In a market economy and in a democracy, no-one should be allowed to become so powerful that he can define the rules of the game. If this happens, he needs to be downsized, just like AT&T or Standard Oil were downsized when their monopolies did too much harm to the people.

A market economy is said to have the capability to distribute wealth quite justly among its people. A capitalistic economy, where a minority of capitalists defines the rules to its advantage, definitely won't do it. It will only make the rich richer.

And America has been moving away from a market economy and approaching capitalism – with most of Europe on its tails. The result is that the rich become richer and the poor become poorer as the rising Gini-coefficient clearly shows.

The reason is that we mistake anarchy for freedom and tolerate that a minority enriches itself by asking for more freedom – and thus taking away the freedom for the majority of the people.

What Can Be Done?

So what can be done? What should we do to change this?

Now that's a question I won't even try to answer. That's up to everyone. All I wanted to show in this short essay was that there really is something going wrong which needs to be changed. And I wanted to give an idea of what might be the reason.

The most important insight is that too much freedom can kill freedom.

This sounds like a ludicrous statement, but I hope I could show that this really is the case. Too much freedom is called anarchy. And it only serves the powerful.

If we really want to create a free society, we need rules. Again, it sounds like a contradiction, but a society without rules, without certain limits to freedom, would be an anarchic society.

Freedom can only survive if everyone can participate. You can tell people that they have the freedom to do as they like, but if they don't have the means and don't even have the possibility to achieve them – what is their freedom really worth? After all, everybody is free to die. Even in the most brutal dictatorship.

Take responsibility for your society, not just for the group you are living in. Remember that others have rights, too. And they would also like to have a decent living. Try to live under Rawls' "veil of ignorance" before you make a decision. It may help to reduce your ignorance.

If we continue to ignore these simple rules, the American Dream might turn into a nightmare for good where man is a wolf to his fellow man.

And this will not only happen in America.

Free Enterprise – Slave Citizens

Free Enterprise

Human beings are an incredibly inventive race. Let them figure out how they can cover a distance of 100 kilometers, and they come up with different solutions like horses, cars, trains, boats or bicycles. Depending on your personal likings or environmental conditions you will pick one of these and use them. If you are athletic, you might choose the bike; if you don't care when exactly you will go and if you don't like driving, you might take the train. Most of us would probably take the car. It's faster than most of the other solutions and you can decide on your own at what time you want to leave.

It's the same with economic systems. You can very well live in a mercantilist state or in a communist country; it doesn't necessarily have to be a market economy. Why not let the government or a ruler decide what should be produced to attain certain political goals?

A mercantilist state used the economy to fight neighboring countries, to keep them down. So it tried to collect as much gold as possible. To achieve that goal, mercantilist economies had to be self-sufficient, i.e. they did not want to import anything from other countries, because then you would have to pay these goods with money, which meant gold in the end. At the same time, mercantilist economies had to be strong so they could export huge amount of products into other countries – and collect their precious gold. This accumulation of gold was meant to increase the strength of the home land. After all you need money to pay an army.

This simple plan has only one slight drawback: If every country adopts that strategy, you end up with countries that don't exchange goods anymore – not even goods they might need because they can only be produced at a low quality in your own country or cannot be produced at all. Just think of lemons growing in Iceland. It might work, but you shouldn't rely on it.

So on the long run mercantilism was doomed – and it finally died out some centuries ago.

Communism followed a similar path; here the state also used the economy to achieve political goals. The economy in a communist country was meant to produce goods that strengthened the state. It was meant to produce steel and guns to assure military independence or even provide the means to attack other countries. And it was meant to collect foreign currencies so the communist states could buy those goods abroad that they weren't able to produce at home. In general, it meant that the communist countries were selling raw materials like natural gas or petroleum on the world market.

In trying to achieve these strategic goals, however, the communist countries forgot a minor detail of their national economy: The consumers. The consumers were never in the focus of the notorious five-year-plans. They somehow had to deal with the leftovers of the planned economy. In the end, there came a time when the people rebelled against the communist regime (not only for the reason that it was much easier to buy bananas in the West then in the East, I acknowledge that). And so communism joined mercantilism on the cemetery of history (with the exception of a very strange country in the east of Asia that managed to establish the first communist dynasty ever).

It was not until the 18th century, that European philosophers came up with a very strange and very unusual idea of what an economy could look like. One of the first of these thinkers – and probably the best known – was the Scottish philosopher Adam Smith who simply asked: Why not let the people handle the economy on their own? Why do we need a centralized government that tells the people what they should produce and how much money they should get for it? Let the people figure this out for themselves!

He published these radical ideas in his famous book "The Wealth of Nations" that was published in 1776, the same year that the USA declared its independence from the British Empire. But as a Scotsman, he probably didn't care about this detail.

His ideas fell on prepared grounds. Liberal ideas were something of a fashion in Europe at that time, when the aristocracy, the rulers of former times, started to lose their grip on the society. Their power was vanishing, even more when the industrial revolution came to full speed in the 19th century. Now you didn't make your money with renting land to poor people, now you made your money with producing goods – and exploiting poor people for doing that.

These cruelties of the first decades, however, were finally overcome, and the free market system – or free enterprise system – could finally show its strength. It provided goods to all people; it provided a certain wealth to all people. Famines that shook national economies on a regular basis became unknown in the industrialized countries and today remind us of legends from times long ago (unless people created them artificially by waging war). Everyone has access to schools and health care. The situation improved significantly in the market economies – especially in comparison to the communist countries, that promised to provide a worker's Paradise on earth but got lost somewhere on their way. The workers in communist countries never came as close to Paradise as the workers in the Western market economies.

A democratic society needs a free economy. You can't guarantee the freedom of speech or free elections and then tell the people what they should produce and to whom they should sell the goods. That wouldn't work. So a free market and democracy go hand in hand.

Living in a democracy means that there is no ruler that tells you what to do; there are rules and laws, but they have been decided by the people for the people and apply to all. The situation is similar in a market economy: It wouldn't work either if there were an absolute ruler that told it what to do. There is no-one that can set the price for a good to a number he likes best. The price is found in a free exchange between the forces of supply and demand, between the enterprise and the customer. If one side had the power to set the price, then the free market would die instantly.

Imagine a butcher that all of a sudden wants to get fifty Euros for a kilogram of meat. If he were the only one, he might get it, although the demand will drop significantly, as only the very rich will be able to pay such a price and buy meat from now on.

But we live in a market economy. There is not just one butcher, there are hundreds. Some might increase the price as they think it's a good idea. But others might even lower the price to attract more customers, because you can also become a millionaire with a small margin, if only the volume sold is big enough. That's the secret of discounters. In the end everyone (including the rich, for why should they pay the higher price?) buys his meat at the cheaper butchers. The expensive butchers either lower their price – or they go bankrupt. In a market economy they don't have the power to enforce the price of a good.

On the other hand, a customer might want to have a kilogram of meat for fifty Cents. If he's lucky, he might find a butcher that sells him meat for such a low price. But it is probably not recommendable to eat it. And he will never find a butcher who sells him meat of a decent quality at such a low price. Also the customer doesn't have the power to enforce his price.

Both a democracy and a market economy find their way by voting. In politics you elect a certain candidate, in a market economy you vote for the price of a product. If the price is too high, the goods won't be bought, neither will they, if the quality is too bad. On the other hand, no company will produce a good if the price the customer wants to pay is too low. At the end the demand- and supply-side come up with production volumes and prices that satisfy everyone.

Capitalism

Free enterprise, market economy, capitalism: We generally believe that these words all mean the same and are just synonyms for the economic system of the Western world. This assumption, however, is not fully correct.

Capitalism and free market developed in parallel, so this might have given the impression that they are identical. But in fact they are promoting different economical systems.

A capitalist seems to be a rather new invention that showed up during the industrial revolution. This was the time when human labor was replaced by machines on a large scale. The difference between the two production systems of human and machine labor is not only that you need the appropriate technology that allows machines to do the work of humans. You also need the money to invest in the machines.

A production that purely relies on humans is rather risk-free. The upfront invest is negligible, if the business doesn't develop as planned you simply fire the workers. The risk of losing money in your business adventure is rather low. All this changes when you use machines. Now you have to make a significant invest upfront and can only hope that your business plan is somewhat realistic and you will get your money back by producing and selling the goods. This risk is taken by the capitalist, as the payback might be significant. But it is a gamble; there is a risk that the capitalist will lose his investment. And if there is one thing all humans have in common, then it is the fact that they don't like to take risks. Whenever they see a possibility to reduce risks, they take this possibility. And there are several possibilities for a capitalist to reduce the risk. One of them is extremely popular among capitalists.

One of the first capitalists were the Fuggers that dominated trade in central Europe in the 15th century (so capitalist existed in fact well before the industrial revolution). They were living in Augsburg, Germany, and had their hands in everything that promised to make them richer. They even invested in mining, and it is said that it was in one of their mines that the word "worker" (Arbeiter in German) was used for the first time.

But mainly they traded. Spices, clothes, gold, salt – there was nothing they wouldn't trade to make money. However, they were not the only traders in Europe. Hundreds of other traders provided a tough competition. And the risk connected with trading exotic goods was extremely high, as the upfront investment was high: You had to provide a ship (or even a small fleet) that would travel around Africa to bring back goods from India and China. In those times, not all of them made it back home, which meant a huge loss for the trader (and for the relatives of the sailors, but history takes only care of really important people). So the risk was high – and the price of the exotic goods would be even higher to cover that risk. In general, they can always be higher, independent of the risk.

The Fuggers, however, had come up with a bright idea how to minimize the risk – or better: How to increase the prices to a level that made sure they would always earn money in their trades, even if losses due to risks increased. The plan was simple: The Fuggers extensively lent money to the monarchs of Europe. At that time, it was very fashionable to attack your neighboring country every second year or so (the Europeans only stopped that tradition at the end of the 20th century), but these adventures were quite expensive. And the probability that a monarch would pay back its debts was low. But the Fuggers didn't mind, because they got something more precious in exchange: They got the monopoly for certain trading goods. Now they could decide on the prices – and could make sure they had a very positive margin on their products. That made them the riches family in Europe at their time (and one of the first who build social housings; the quarter is still existing in Augsburg, and as the last Fugger forgot to mention that the rent should be increased once in a while the rent is ludicrously low today. But you have to pray several times per day for the soul of the Fuggers if you want to live in these apartments. They probably had a feeling that their economic behavior wasn't quite moral.)

As this example shows, every capitalist has only one goal: He is trying to get a monopoly for his products to make sure that his investments will pay back. And this did not only happen at the end of the Middle Ages.

At the beginning of the 20th century, the Swedish entrepreneur Ivar Kreuger had a similar plan: He lent money to the countries of Europe that were weakened by the First World War (although they didn't know at that time that it was the first), and in exchange he got a monopoly for matches. His company was the only company that could sell matches in many European countries, including Germany, where the monopoly only ended in the 1980s. In the times before lighters, such a monopoly was almost like printing money.

Unfortunately for Kreuger, it was only *almost* like printing money. When the European countries defaulted on their debt during the recession of the 1930s, his empire crumbled and Kreuger committed suicide.

Or look at Microsoft. How many times have the authorities looked into the business practice of this company because it abused its market power? It was this market power that made Microsoft's Internet Explorer the most used browser and that provided a deadly blow to the Netscape Navigator that started it all.

Another story is AT&T, the almighty telephone company that was split up at the beginning of the 1980s because it had abused its monopoly status. Or remember Standard Oil, the oil company that was founded by John D. Rockefeller. The company practically controlled the oil-business in the USA around 1900. And it hadn't shown much scruple to become number one in the market. If a competitor didn't want to sell his drill hole for a ludicrously low price offered by Standard Oil, it could very well happen that the hole exploded the very next day and the competitor was out of business.

Capitalists like to dominate the market. That is the only way they can be sure that their investment will pay off. And the successful ones don't care much about rules and regulations. Reaching their goal of being number one is the only rule that counts.

And that's where we have the difference to a market economy. Capitalism is comparable to a dictatorship – every capitalist tries to dominate its market. A market economy, on the other hand, is comparable to democracy. A democracy is defined by a set of rules that everyone has to follow. Everyone is equal in a democracy; there is not one group that can claim a certain set of rules for itself while the rest of the population has to follow different rules. A democracy treats everyone equally, that's why Lady Justice is blind. A dictatorship or oligarchy, on the other hand, privileges a small group of people.

This brings us to the conclusion that capitalism and a market economy are deadly enemies, like communism and democracy. They are incompatible.

The English language created the expression of "free enterprise", which is revealing. In political and economical discussions, free enterprise shall mean the same as "market economy". An economy that is free from any governmental interference, a liberal economy that is compatible to a democratic political system.

But the expression "free enterprise" stresses the freedom of the companies. The important point seems to be that companies have the freedom to do as they wish. But the economy is more than just companies; it is more than just the supply side. There are also the customers; there is also the demand-side.

But if you stress the freedom of one side, the scales get imbalanced. If you assure the complete freedom of one side, you will restrict the freedom of the other side.

Imagine two people living together. This will only work if both of them follow certain rules of behavior. If one of them misbehaves all the time, the other one will suffer. If one of them takes what he wants, acts as he wants, then the other one can follow his example and this will end in a kind of war, or the other one can silently endure his sufferings. But this will restrict his freedom; it will make him a slave to the first one.

If we want companies to get all the freedom they need, we accept that we restrict the freedom of the customers, of the people.

And in fact, that's what's happening in the Western world today.

The Power of Companies

The sheer size of some companies is simply breath-taking. If you just take the number of employees, the American retailer Walmart is by far the biggest company in the world with roughly 2.2 million employees (all numbers from 2010). Some Chinese oil-companies like Sinopec or China National Petroleum have more than 1 million employees, the majority of the big Fortune 500 companies, however, has some 100,000 employees, like Volkswagen with 500,000 employees, Gazprom with 400,000 employees or Toyota with 325,000 employees. Just the number of employees would fill a mid-sized city – and there are even more people depending on the well-being of these companies. They belong to the family of the employees or are working for the suppliers of the giants, because many companies have outsourced part of their production to save costs. Apple seems to be the most successful company with this respect. At half the revenue of Volkswagen it only employs one eight of the people, or 63,000.

Nevertheless, the revenue of roughly 100 billion dollars for Apple is quite a number, especially as they gained 26 billion dollars in 2010. This high gain is only topped by energy companies like the Royal Dutch Shell (31 billion with revenues of 484 billion dollars), ExxonMobil (41 of 452), or Gazprom that proved to be the most successful company on the list, generating gains of 44 billion with revenues of only 155 billion.

Even though Apple's revenues were significantly lower than ExxonMobil's, they were number one when it came to market capitalization in 2010, with a large margin before ExxonMobil. Apple was worth 559 billion dollars, ExxonMobil on second place had only a value of 408 billion dollars. In all, 51 companies had market capitalizations of more than 100 billion dollars; while 65 had revenues higher than 100 billion Euros, and 31 companies earned more than 10 billion dollars in 2010 (this only covers companies listed on the stock market).

On the other hand, from the 187 countries of which data are available, only 61 had a gross domestic product of more than100 billion dollars. Only 27 countries had a gross domestic product that was bigger than the revenues generated by Shell. And only 20 countries were worth more than Apple (if you assume that the GDP is the value of the country).

If you consider that money is power, these numbers should make you wonder how powerful these international companies really are. And there are more numbers that could make you nervous:

If you sum up all the money all the countries of the world are spending on school and university education, and if you divide this number by two, you get the amount of money only the transnational companies like General Electric and Coca-Cola are spending on advertisement. This doesn't account for national companies that are also spending a lot of money to convince customers to buy their products.

But now you might understand why Shakespeare's sonnets, Moliere's comedies, Goethe's tragedies or simple physical laws are mostly unknown to the younger generation, whereas they do not have a problem to identify a product after having heard only a few notes of the music used in advertisements on television. After all, a good education needs a lot of money.

Pharmaceutical companies probably came to the same conclusion. That's why they are spending more on advertising in the USA alone than all American medical schools are spending on educating their students.

I hope that after having presented these numbers, you are convinced that there is a lot of money at stake when dealing with huge companies. They easily surpass smaller countries in their wealth and thus in their potential power. But power alone is not a bad thing. It depends on how you use it. We remember Uncle Ben saying to his nephew Peter Parker in the first Spiderman-movie: "With great power comes great responsibility."

Spiderman is powerful, Superman is even more powerful, and they both use their strength with great responsibility. But they are cartoon characters. In reality, the situation might be somewhat different. Lord Acton, who lived in the 19th century, is quoted for having said:

"Power tends to corrupt, and absolute power corrupts absolutely. Great men are almost always bad men."

This is in direct contradiction to the dogma of neo-liberal economics that likes to quote Adam Smith who assured us that even though the rich might act selfishly, they are guided by an invisible hand with the results that the wealth will be distributed justly among the rich and the poor.

John Maynard Keynes commented this understanding of his fellow economist with the words: "Capitalism is the astounding belief that the most wickedest of men will do the most wickedest of things for the greatest good of everyone."

And he might have been right – just like Lord Acton. This comes as a bit of a surprise, because Lord Acton as well as John Keynes were offspring of the upper class. But they should know best what to expect of their kind.

In fact, companies don't have a tendency to care much about their employees. Yes, I know, there is a lot being said about work-life-balance and being attractive to employees. But as soon as the camera is turned off, the company behaves like an Alzheimer patient, forgets all it has said just minutes ago, fires the employees in "expensive" countries and hires new employees in low cost countries.

And low cost does not only mean low wages. It means low costs for the production in general, because they don't have to care about environmental, security, social or any other regulations. They can do as they like. Well, they are free enterprises, aren't they?

So when they are looking for a place to open a new production site that will create hundreds or even thousands of jobs, they do not ask if they will have a nice view from the production site, say, over a well protected and completely unharmed forest; or they do not ask if there are nice restaurants and clean streets around the production side. All that matters are costs. So they look at the wages, they look at the taxes and they look at regulations that might increase the costs of production like the necessity to recycle the waste because they are not allow to dump it into the next river. All these factors matter, nothing else.

You could argue that companies do not only look at these features, why else would they invest in the USA or in

Germany? Maybe there are other factors that are also of some importance. But don't forget: Companies like BMW or Mercedes that created new production lines in the USA did this in the south, not in the north, where they would have to deal with the unions. Wages in the south of the USA are much lower – and thus more attractive to investors. The picture in Germany seems to be similar. Only that the Germans were able to distribute their low wage worker's class evenly trough-out the country.

The companies are looking for the countries with the lowest social and environmental levels. When a country tries to lift these levels by introducing environmental regulations or higher minimum wages, the investors move on. These was experienced by the so-called "Tiger-states" in Asia, countries like Malaysia and Thailand that once were the favorites of the investors, until their wealth grew and they came up with the funny idea that they should increase the social status of the whole population, so it can benefit from the rising wealth. And it is being experienced by China, which is raising its minimum wage – and cloth producers are now moving to Bangladesh, as the wages are much lower there.

Thank God there was no globalization in place when the workers in Europe and the USA demanded their rights and fought – successfully – for higher wages. The companies couldn't simply move to other countries and the population had the chance to enjoy some luxury for some time – before the globalization set in and removed it again.

As every country tries to please the rich investors – after all low wages are better than no wages – they are competing for the lowest standards. Of course, it is their free decision to do this. They could also decide to ignore the wishes of the companies and live in poverty (continuing or as a new experience). It's their free choice.

No, really, it isn't. It's blackmail. The companies have taken the employees as their hostages and are dictating the rules of the game.

Companies Define the Rules

Living in a community means that you have to follow certain rules. One of the earliest – and probably simplest – laws were the Ten Commandments of the Old Testament. "Thou shalt not kill" and "thou shalt not steal" are rules that have been valid for every human society since millennia.

Over the time, the law books became thicker, more complicated and not necessarily more logical. But still there are some basic rules that everybody accepts. These include, of course, the interdiction of killing and stealing. But today's laws also guarantee human rights, they protect us against fraud, they protect our health against selfish actions of some who value a few dollars higher than human life, and they ask everyone to contribute to the financing of our society, i.e. to pay taxes. And in a democratic society, these rules are valid for everyone.

Well, as we used to say about communism and its leaders: There are always some who are more equal. There are always some who behave as if the laws of our society didn't apply to them.

One prominent example is the company that had the highest market capitalization worldwide in 2012: Apple. Once upon a time, Apple simply decided that it would continue to profit from the infrastructure, security, social system and life-quality of the countries it is active in, but didn't really want to participate in the costs. To put it short:

They simply decided that paying taxes according to the rules would not be appropriate for a company of their success and reputation.

To be fair: They are not the only company that tries to avoid taxes wherever it can. But they were the most prominent example at the time these lines were written; and they were probably the most successful company when it came to avoiding taxes.

The tricks company like Apple are using are always similar: Look for incompatibilities in the worldwide tax laws. One often used hole is an incompatibility between Irish and American tax laws. According to Irish tax laws a company has to pay taxes in the country where the company is managed. According to American tax laws a company has to pay taxes in the country it has been founded. That doesn't look like an incompatibility of laws and a possibility for companies like Apple to avoid taxes. After all, Apple was founded in the USA and is managed from the USA. So situation is clear: Apple has to pay taxes in the USA, according to American laws.

But paying taxes is not in the interest of Apple. Like any capitalist, they want to maximize the gains, and one way to maximize the gains is to reduce the costs like taxes. So Apple founded a subsidiary, the Apple Sales International (ASI) in Ireland. As this company has been founded in Ireland, it doesn't have to pay taxes in the USA according to American laws. Still better: ASI may exist in Ireland, but Apple pretends it is being managed from the USA. So ASI doesn't have to pay taxes in Ireland according to Irish laws.

Now Apple owns a company that doesn't have to pay taxes neither in the USA nor in Ireland. That turned it into a gemstone in the Apple universe, and it quickly became its center: All goods produced in China by Apples subcontractors are not bought by Apples to be sold by

Apple, but they are bought by ASI to be sold by Apple. ASI is buying the iPhone, iPods and iPads from companies like Foxconn in China and sells them to the Apple stores and other retailers to a much higher price. Thus, ASI is gaining a lot of money. And it doesn't have to pay taxes in any country. Ka-Ching!

In fact, Apple's model is a little bit more complicated than described, as the American government was well aware of this hole and tried to close it. But if you use a whole bunch of subsidiaries to transfer money in-between, even the best tax-inspector gets lost – and the company can keep its money.

Be aware: Everything Apple does is completely legal. It was only not intended to be legal. But you need some basic moral sentiment to understand this and resist the temptation to fool the government and your fellow citizens. But companies like Apple and their management don't get pay for moral sentiments.

In the end, Apple's approach to avoiding taxes was extremely successful. Instead of the 35 percent tax rate for companies that it would have to pay in the USA, Apple actually paid less than one tenth of a percent per year in the last years. Instead of billions, they only pay about ten million dollars of taxes.

The main idea is copied by all international companies: They simply shift goods internally from one subsidiary to another and assign random prices to these goods that have the only effect that the gains end up in those countries which have the lowest tax rates. It is no joke, but more than half of the world-trade that is meant to improve the life of the customers is in fact taking place within giant enterprises that shift goods from one production- or sales-site to another.

Sometimes not even goods are shifted from one country to another country, but also intellectual property rights. This includes the brand-name and logo, but also patents or copyrights. They are generally transferred to subsidiaries in the Netherlands, and these companies are then licensing the right to use a patent or the company logo to the other subsidiaries of the company. Why such a complicated setup? Because the Netherlands don't tax incomes made from royalties. This model is not only used by companies like Google or IKEA. Also the rock-group U2 collected the copyrights of its songs in a Dutch company – and reduced the low tax rates of their home-country Ireland even further. Google achieved to reduce its tax rate to only 3 percent with such tricks – still much higher than Apple, but way too low to be fair.

With tricks like this, huge companies manage to reduce their taxes by an estimated 1000 billion Euros only in Europe. The European debt crises would not be a topic if companies would play fair.

This behavior is not only unfair towards its fellow citizens and the community. After all, companies like Apple are not an island far away from the state. They depend on the state and its institutions like everyone else. Even more so: Their business is based on their ideas, their inventions, the unique design of their products, the customer-friendly user interfaces, certain technologies. They need a strong state that protects their intellectual property again idea-thefts and against counterfeit. They need a strong state that helps them to protect their intellectual property. If anyone were able to copy Apple products as they liked, Apple wouldn't need such sophisticated tricks to avoid taxes. They would pay only a few million in taxes because their gains were less miraculous.

So Apple expects the state to protect its business – but is not willing to participate in the financing of the state. They take all they can get – but are not willing to pay for it. The moral rules of living in a community are not for them. Companies like Apple live outside of the laws that apply for everyone else.

These laws especially apply to smaller companies that don't have the means to construct such complicated financial architectures to avoid taxes. You need an international foothold to be able to set up subsidiaries in several countries. And you need a lot of lawyers and tax consultant that look for the holes in the international tax laws and construct legally sound solutions to avoid taxes (at least these consultants get their money).

A small company could never come up with a solution like Apple or other international companies that only pay a fraction of the taxes they should be paying. A small company is paying the whole sum of taxes, no discount attached. But by following the law, these companies are less competitive than international tricksters. They have to demand higher prices or can spend less money on innovation for the next product generation. While the international companies are doing well, the smaller ones are losing the battle. The big companies are growing while the smaller ones are dying.

With their immoral behavior, the big companies are defining the rules of the game.

*

Companies, not only the big ones, are constantly trying to take control of the game that we call economy. Other examples are the ways companies are trying to hide information from the customers.

When you go to a butcher (if you still find one and he hasn't been replaced by an anonymous supermarket), you are convinced that he is selling you a nice piece of meat. When you are going to a fishmonger, you are convinced to get a nice filet of fish from fish captured in the wild sea. Well, that might be the case. But sometimes there is more behind.

The piece of meat could be from a lucky cow that was grazing on endless grasslands before it was quickly killed by a butcher that is preparing the meat with all the skills of his profession. But in most cases, the cow was grown in a huge barn with hundreds of others, having not enough space to move, standing on one spot throughout its short live, getting chemical additives in its food that are meant to increase the speed of its growth and to protect it against illnesses that are common in environments like this where you hundreds of cows are locked up in a small space.

Some say that this chemical cocktail might also help to keep the meat fresh for a longer time, but that is probably due to other chemical additives the meat is treated with after is has been slaughter by unskilled workers in a factory that, at least in Germany, generally come from poor East-European countries and are happy to work for wages that are less than one tenth of the average income in Germany.

The fish that you find on the table probably has never seen the wild sea, but only breeding facilities where they have been enclosed with hundreds of their kind. Some say that animals don't mind being sandwiched for all their life, because they don't feel like humans do. But this probably only means that animals have feelings.

And like cows, the fish also get a lot of chemicals that help them to grow and stay healthy in an unhealthy environment. But unlike cows, food technology has found a way to reduce the chemical burden of dead fish: The producers put them in an alkaline solution which increases the water content of fish by up to 40 percent – and thus reduces the average chemical burden of what used to be fish meat.

You might be shocked to hear about these things, but don't worry: You will never know if your food was contaminated or treated this way, because the companies won't tell you. You can guess that the quality is low if the price is very low, but you can never be sure that the quality is high if the price is high.

And if the information is available that there is something wrong with your food: Don't worry. You will probably miss that piece of information in all the information that's being dumped on you during the day. And the TV shows that you have to watch to see what really happened to doctor… whomever. Include a name or replace doctor by detective or lover or… The industry doesn't inform us, but it entertains as well. We are "Amusing Ourselves to Death" as Neil Postman wrote in the 1980s. But that was a long time ago. By now, we are already zombies.

Otherwise it is unexplainable why we are still using artificial sweeteners. You probably think that the reason should be obvious: We eat a lot of fat and a lot of sugar (more than any other human generation was able to eat in the history of mankind) and look at the results: Many humans resemble little globes that seem to orbit around the earth. Men used to hunt animals, to follow their trails for hours, now they're often too heavy and too lazy to make it from the TV to the fridge, so they put the TV next to it. Exchanging sugar with calorie-free sweeteners seems to be a good idea to reduce the weight of the overweight.

Only it isn't.

Sweeteners are also very popular with farmers. Not because they are too fat as well (they still have to do a lot of physical work which for some reasons seems to help against cushion-like pads of fat on the body), but because they like their animals fat. They add sweeteners to the food of their pigs, and the pigs gain weight faster than without them. Sweeteners are the perfect product to fatten animals.

Okay, that sounds lunatic. But the truth is sometimes unbelievable. And the fact is that the calorie-free sweeteners help to fatten pigs. And not only pigs: they are also quite successful with another, this time bipedal omnivore.

The explanation is simple: When you eat or drink something that contains an artificial sweetener, your gustative nerves send the signal "sweet" to your brain. Your brain has been conditioned in thousands of years of evolution, and it knows very well that this means that sugar has entered the stomach. So the body starts to produce insulin to metabolize the sugar. Large quantities of this hormone are released into the bloodstream to metabolize sugar. Only there was no sugar in your food. Our stupid brain is still not used to the fact that our food technology allows us to produce flavors without contents. But insulin cannot just be removed from the blood, so it metabolizes the sugar it finds in the blood. The result is that you get hungry again – and eat more, and more, and more... And if you are a big consumer of sweeteners, your appetite and finally your external circumference will grow accordingly. And you thought sweeteners would help you to reduce your weight…

In addition, sweeteners can also be bad to your health in other respects. One of the most popular sweeteners today is Aspartame. It is sold e.g. under the name NutraSweet. The Searle Company, later bought by Monsanto, tried to introduce Aspartame to the market already in the 1970s. However, even while the FDA was still reviewing Searle's application for release, rumors came up that Aspartame might cause brain tumors. The FDA was uneasy about this and requested more studies. The FDA even found out that Searle manipulated several studies it had presented to the FDA so that Aspartame would look healthier than it actually was. Finally the FDA came to the conclusion that Aspartame should not be released until it was clear that it was not dangerous for humans.

Fortunately for Searle, whose CEO Donald Rumsfeld was and old Republican politician, the American people elected Ronald Reagan as the new president at the beginning of the 1980s; he appointed a new head to the FDA who was less critical than his colleagues and single-handedly released Aspartame.

And what did the Europeans do? Well, they didn't bother to conduct their own studies. They looked at the American decision and simply copied it.

Today, there are speculations that Aspartame might not only be carcinogenic, but also hazardous to the nervous system. But as Monsanto was never really interesting in finding out, no research group was sponsored to take a closer look at the topic. So we can only speculate.

We can also only speculate about the dangers of genetic engineering. The official understanding of companies and governments in the USA and quite often also in Europe is that genetically modified organisms don't present any danger to the health of the consumers. The companies have introduced genes to make their crop more resistant to pesticides, or they have introduced genes so that plants produce a certain poison that protects them against vermin but is harmless to humans. As these genes can also be found in other plants or animals and are not dangerous to humans – this has been proven quite convincingly – neither the gen-companies like Monsanto nor several governmental officials seem to understand why there is such a resistance against genetic engineering, especially in Europe.

Don't these critics understand? All the gen-companies did was to take a DNA-sequence from one living organism and to introduce it into another organism. They didn't come up with a DNA-sequence of their own that has not been available before in Mother Nature! The DNA-sequence as well as the protein it codes have been available for millions of years, so why the fear about genetic engineering?

Sounds convincing, doesn't it? Unfortunately, it's only part of the story. You are not supposed to hear the whole story, but here it is:

The picture the industry wants to draw is that one DNA-sequence codes on protein, that there is a one-to-one translation like for the English word "cow" which means "Kuh" in German, and both make you think of milk. That is only partly correct. As with words, the true translation depends on the context. If you put a DNA-sequence in some places of the DNA, it can code the protein, just as cow can be translated with Kuh, and both describe a milk-producing animal. But if you add "dopey" to cow in English or "bloede" to "Kuh" in German, you have an insult addressed to humans and no longer the description of an animal. Similarly: integrating the same DNA-sequence into another part of the DNA can prompt the genes to produce a completely different protein, or to not produce a certain protein at all or to do something completely different. There is no one-to-one translation for a DNA into a protein, the context, the position of the sequence in the genes matters.

But, you might wonder, of cause the genetic engineers can control where the new DNA sequence will be incorporated in the genes. Judge for yourself: A very popular way to introduce new DNA into the cell nucleus is to attach them to gold-nanoparticles and shoot these particles with a so called "gene-guns" into the nucleus. Do you think that this procedure allows you to define the exact position of the DNA-sequence inside the genes? They just end up anywhere. And other methods are not any more precise.

The DNA-sequence will end up anywhere within the genes and can control any behavior and not just the production of the desired protein. And this is what happens. If you test genetically engineered crops you will find that their protein-content is not identical to the content of the natural plant. And this is true not only for the protein that was modified consciously. Or the plants have a lower yield than their natural counterpart, or can suddenly grow at lower temperatures – what was never intended –, or grow two or three corn cobs where only one corn cob should grow.

The list of unexpected behavior of genetically modified organisms is seemingly endless. Anything can happen and you will never know what unless you really tested for it. But as the official statement is that one DNA-sequence codes one protein and other behavior cannot be expected, only a minority of researchers performs these experiments. It is only a minority, because they don't get paid by the companies (as they could only lose) or by the state (as it thinks there is no question that needs to be answered). So they have to find the money for their experiments elsewhere. But the results are disturbing: Genetically engineered food seems to be dangerous for humans. It can be carcinogenic, and it is treated by the immune system like an illness, like a foreign body, and not like food. Of course these findings are preliminary. It would require further studies to assure these findings. But no-one seems to be interested: The company make a lot of money with genetically modified organisms, and the state likes companies that make a lot of money. After all, enterprises are free.

They don't have to tell us what they are doing. It seems to be never required, until someone finds out that what they are doing is really dangerous. Up to this point, we believe that what they are doing will be okay. After all, they are creating jobs and at least the employees are paying taxes. That's all our government wants to know.

Thus it allows even obviously dangerous processes like "fracking" or hydraulic fracturing. Fracking seems to be a smart idea to get the last drop of petroleum or natural gas out off the soil. The process seems to be simple: Just take some water, add a little bit of sand and some chemicals and inject the mixture under high pressure into the soil. This will cause small fractures underground along which the petroleum or gas moves towards the well and can be collected.

Fracking is a promising technology. It allows to access large oil and natural gas occurrences that would have been inaccessible without fracking. Some predict that thanks to fracking the USA will be exporting oil again in some decades. Old predictions that the oil supply should be exhausted by the middle of this century now look as reliable as the prophecies made by Nostradamus.

There still will be an end to the petroleum age. But it's now so far away – so why should be care?

Well, we might want to care because all the petroleum and natural gas that we are burning increases the amount of carbon dioxide in our atmosphere. And this leads to the climate change even though the fossil fuel industry does all it can to question the connection between more carbon dioxide and rising temperatures.

But again: Why should we care? We might already see some impact of the climate change today, but the real tough times are far away in the future. Some of us might not even be alive anymore to experience it. Okay, ours kids will still be on earth and suffer from it, but think of all the money we can make today!

Apart from those gloomy speculations about a dark future that seems to be so misplaced if the present looks bright, there are also some dark spots related to fracking that we can observe today.

The process of fracking requires water and chemicals to be injected into the soil. We can't see what's going on below the ground, but although it's out of sight, it has a huge impact on our daily life; because we depend on the ground water as our drinking water.

The industry tells us that there is no risk at all that the ground water will be affected by fracking. This process is taking place well below the layers that contain the ground water. So how could fracking possibly affect the ground water?

I can't answer that. But the fact is: It does.

There are two source of contamination. One is the natural gas that has been released through fracking. It is not only moving towards the drilling well, but also towards the ground water. It mixes with the ground water. Now, if you use that ground water as drinking water, you can make a nice experiment: Just open the water-tap and bring a flame close to the flowing water. The water will start to burn!

Of course, it isn't the water that's burning, it's the natural gas trapped in the water. But it looks impressive nevertheless. And there are hundreds of homes in America that can show you the miracle of burning water. And of having a supply of drinking water that you shouldn't drink.

In other regions where the industry uses fracking, the drinking water shouldn't be drunk as well. But here the reason is that it became contaminated with the chemicals contained in the mixture used for fracking. It shouldn't happen that these chemicals contaminate the ground water, but it shouldn't happen that nuclear power plants just explode, either. Nature doesn't always play to our likings or mathematical theories.

So some farmers in America that depend on their ground wells for water supply nowadays get their drinking water by car. Once a week a lorry sponsored by the oil industry passes by and leaves some gallons of water behind, as the water in the well shouldn't be drunk. It is simply too dangerous.

The industry, however, will not really tell why it is dangerous, because they don't even tell us which chemicals are used for the fracking process. Some are known and frightening because they are carcinogenic, but a large number of those chemicals are simply "company confidential". Even the authorities don't know what the mixtures contain.

Imagine that someone brings a food on the market but doesn't tell anyone what it contains, or a medicine whose components are completely unknown. The customer doesn't know what he is consuming. Do you think that should be allowed?

In fact, that was allowed until the beginning of the twentieth century. At this time, the chemical industry came up with a lot of nice artificial additives for nutrition and medicine that were used amply by the industry. No-one knew about their danger – and many consumers had to find out the hard way that there were some. After several people had died the authorities installed institutions that oversee the release of new substances for human consumption. There is still a risk that something goes wrong, but the risk is lower than before when no-one was watching.

And now the industry is using the fracking process, and no-one is watching again. But to be fair: The chemicals used during fracking are not meant for human consumption.

They are just released into our soil where they might end up in the ground water or even in the top soil that nourishes the plants we eat.

So the chemicals might end up in our food nevertheless. Only the industry and the authorities think it will never happen – and close their eyes to these cases where it did happen. As if things didn't exist that you don't see. And as they don't exist, there is no need to find out what chemicals the industry is pumping underground. If we knew, we might have to restrict their usage, and that would be in sharp contradiction to our economic system of *free* enterprise.

Again, you have to choose between capitalism and market economy. Capitalists want to gain as much advantage from their investment as they can. They don't want you to know what you are really buying, just trust them that it is really good and will never ever cause a problem. In the best of all worlds you wouldn't know a thing about the products you are buying, you would solely rely on the word of the capitalist that everything is alright. At least that will make sure that his profits will be alright.

But if you have to trust the capitalist, the supply side, that the quality of the product is really as he promises, he can define the price for it. You can't argue that there are several problems with the product so a lower price would be more adequate, because you don't know. This is, of course, what a capitalist wants. But it ends in a monopoly, it is not a market economy anymore, it destroys the market.

This is a general problem that has been observed by many economists in the last decades (and seems to have been ignored by even more economist and most of our politicians): If the information is not freely available to both sides of the market – the supply side and the demand side – then the market will cease to exist because it is impossible to find the market price. In case of asymmetric information, as the economists call this phenomenon, one side has an advantage and can set the price; this side acts like a monopoly, and the market ceases to exist.

This asymmetric information is a basic problem of our times. The industry has the advantage. It knows where a product has been produced, under which conditions (e.g. child labor or which chemicals have been used), and it knows the dangers associated with it – or at least it knows that there might be a danger but it's better not to know more.

The consumers are kept stupid. We are allowed to see the shiny product, and to watch the entertaining ads, but we better don't know anything really important about the product.

The trousers can be produced by workers that earn decent wages and have at least some social security, or they can be produced by kids working twelve hours a day without any social security and wages so low that they are barely measurable.

The food we are eating can be healthy as Mother Nature intended, or it can be treated with dozens of artificial flavors, preservatives and pesticides.

The energy we are using can be produced in a sustainable way that doesn't put our kids' future in danger, or it can be produced in old-fashioned power-stations that produce more smog than energy and even put our today's life in danger.

In most cases, we don't know the answers, because the industry doesn't tell us. In some cases we can assume the answer, because the state has dared to restrict the freedom of the enterprises (those bloody communists!) and introduced some regulations that e.g. make it illegal in

Europe and the USA to generate electrical power from fossil fuels in power stations that produce too much smog.

But generally, the consumers are left ignorant. Then the market ceases to exist. And that is exactly what the industry is trying to achieve, because then it can dominate the market.

And to assure that a government might not want to introduce some regulations that would provide additional information to the customer, the companies even take control of the government.

Companies are the Rulers

We have companies that are wealthier than most countries of the world. We have companies that pretend to follow the rules and then evade them and hide their money from the state instead of paying their share of the costs. And we have companies that praise the market economy and are the first to strike the deadly blow against it by hiding important information from their customers and thus increasing asymmetric information.

If you try to raise a child, you have to make sure you teach it some moral values. It cannot simply act as it would like to act. Such a behavior would be selfish and we don't tolerate it. Even more: if a child can act as it would like to act, it finally takes over the control of the family. Father and mother are nothing more than slaves to the child, obeying every fancy of their kid. These things are happening; there are many spoiled kids out there. But it is not in the interest of the parents, nor in the interest of the society to raise selfish and spoiled kids. The line between bad behavior and criminal behavior is only a small line.

We have the same problem, which we have with some kids, also with some companies. Their main behavior may not be illegal. But it is immoral and we don't like it. And the step to a completely illegal behavior is just a small step that is only too often made, as history tells us.

One example is the German industry giant Siemens that had some accounts with dirty money it was using to bribe important decision makers all over the world. The investigation of the scandal revealed that even members of Siemens' anti-corruption unit, who were supposed to fights such activities, were involved in the scandal.

Goldman Sachs was selling derivates on mortgages, those "weapons of mass destruction" (as the investor-legend Warren Buffet called them), that caused the most severe financial crisis of the last decades. But they were not only selling these weapons. In 2007, one year before the great meltdown, they constructed a new derivative with the nice name "Abacus" together with the hedge fund manager John Paulson. They sold it to their customers as a good opportunity for investment – and at the same time bet that it would fail which it finally did. Paulson made several billion dollars in this bet.

The list of scandals that show us how easily companies cross the line between bad behavior and criminal behavior is endless. Spending more time with such examples would only lead to high blood pressure and the bitter taste that humans are a rotten race. But these feelings are only signs of our impotent anger. So let's be productive and ask how we can solve the problem. How can we teach companies and their managers how to behave?

If your child misbehaves, the parents are responsible and have to make sure it changes its behavior. If a member (and a powerful member) of the society misbehaves, the society has to deal with it, i.e. the state. The authorities have to make sure that companies behave. The only problem is: Some companies are not only more powerful than the authorities, and they are not only in the position to hide information from the authorities; some companies are in fact the state.

This is a very sobering statement. And it shows us that the answer to our question might be more difficult than even pessimists would have imagined.

But there has always been a tradition – especially in countries like the USA and France – that top managers from companies take over high positions in the government or important authorities, while top politicians or bureaucrats take over high positions in companies. There is revolving door between the administration and companies.

This revolving door is well-known politics in France. The elite school "École nationale d'administration" (National school of administration, ENA) requires that the alumni work for ten years in the administration (of course on highest level) before they can move to another job, which generally is a well paid over top positions in the management of companies like Airbus, Air France, EADS, Peugeot or France Telecom. Practically every important company in France has several ENA-alumni in its managing board. They make sure that the companies act in the interest of France – and that France acts in the interest of the companies. The population has the right to vote, but let's be serious: You never believed that this would change anything, did you?

The situation is less obvious but nevertheless quite similar in the "land of the free". There is not one school that guarantees top positions in the administration or enterprises. But there are some high class universities like Stanford and Harvard that provide the main supply of top managers and politicians in the USA. Of course, these universities and schools are not only for the rich. You can get a scholarship if your marks are good enough. And you won't be allowed to learn at these schools if you are an idiot (or maybe only if you are a very, very rich idiot). But being born in a rich family makes it so much easier to have a good education that allows you to pass the entry tests with ease than being born in a slum where the only things to read are the traffic signs.

So you end up with a practically closed society of rich people that makes sure their kids get good positions in companies or the administration, and the few examples that show us that even poor kids can make it to the very top are the exception not the rule.

And this is not only true for countries like France (ENA), USA (Harvard and Stanford) or the UK (Oxford and Cambridge) where everyone knows the names of the elite schools and universities that will guarantee their alumni a life in top-positions and luxury. This is also true in countries like Germany which seems to be devoid of elite schools. But don't be mistaken: There is not only a "social fracture" as the former French president Jacques Chirac once called it in France, there is also a "social fracture" in Germany.

After the Second World War it might have been possible for everyone to succeed. The federal cabinet of the first great coalition at the end of the sixties (that is the coalition between the social-democrats and the Christian democrats) included members of all social classes. You could find the son of a saleswoman, the son of a butcher or the son of a clerk (okay, you couldn't find the *daughter* of someone in this cabinet; all was not fair in past times).

The federal cabinet of the second grand coalition beginning of the 21st century was less equal. Most positions were taken by kids of the upper class, the bourgeoisie. The same observation can also be made in the managing boards of the companies. It might have been the case that someone starts his career at the age of sixteen with a traineeship in a company, learning how to wire cables, and then steadily moves up the ladder to the position of the CEO. But today, most CEOs have taken the short cut: They come from the upper class, entered the company already in top positions and took over the full control only some years after their first appearance at the company.

About 80 percent of the CEOs of the 100 biggest companies in Germany have made this career; they are sons of the bourgeoisie, whose fathers have been top managers or entrepreneurs or top bureaucrats. The rich form a closed society in our nations. They move from top-position to top-position and don't really make a difference between the interests of the state or the interest of the company. As Charles E. Wilson, CEO of General Motors and then minister of defense in the cabinet of President Eisenhower once said: What's good for the country is good for GM – and vice versa.

Nothing could describe the mindset of our elite better than this statement. And as the responsible persons only move within their circles, they don't really understand that there is more to the country than rich and powerful people. They tend to forget the man on the street, even when they came from the street like the former German Chancellor Gerhard Schröder. Once they reach the top, they strive to please the elite. So the administration Schröder realized the most anti-social laws ever passed in Germany. And today he is a top-manager in the Gazprom group and a well-paid consultant for numerous other companies. The jester made a good job, the jester may live.

Like cancer, the companies and their managers have taken over the body of our state. But even though they occupy many important positions, they cannot occupy every important position. So they have to make sure that the people in control do as they wish.

*

If you cannot take control, you have to make sure that those in control act as you want them to act. To achieve this goal, companies use lobbyist that help them to convince decision-makers.

The word "lobbyist" was first coined in the 19th century in the USA. It comes from the word "lobby" where the company-representatives were waiting for the decision makers to talk to them and to convince them that a certain political decision would be the right one. Lobbying improved since that time: Lobbyists do no longer way in the lobby, but they are residing in sumptuous palaces that are meant to impress.

One of the first and most successful lobby-organizations was the "National Association of Manufacturers" (NAM). This organization represented 35,000 companies like AT&T, DuPont, General Motors, IBM, Johnson & Johnson and Procter & Gamble with more than 5 million employees only in the USA.

The goal of this organization was to create a certain understanding in the population what the role of companies should be in the society. The organization was founded in the 1930s, during the Great Depression where the acceptance of a free economy was low and the hope was high that an economy that was guided by a state (not necessarily controlled as in the communist countries) would solve all economic problems. After all: The free economy without any governmental interference had caused the Great Depression.

The NAM wanted to change that perception. Their key message was that everything would be alright if only the companies were doing well, just like Charles E. Wilson mentioned it some years later. "Free enterprise" should be understood in the sense of "capitalism", i.e. all rights for the companies, and not in the sense of "market economy", i.e. equal rights to all.

And the NAM had an enormous budget to spread this message. They spent millions of dollars for advertisements in newspapers, on billboards, in the radio and in the cinema (there was no television at that time). And they sent their representative into schools, to priests and other opinion leaders. Just one campaign in the late 1940s cost the NAM more than 3 million dollars (which is about 30 million in today's value). But money didn't matter.

Now if we look at the understanding of the role of companies in our society, we can assert that the money spent by the "National Association of Manufacturers" wasn't wasted.

In Germany, an organization that tries to influence the public perception of companies in a similar way was founded only in the year 1999. It is called "Initiative Neue Soziale Marktwirtschaft" (Initiative for a new social market economy, INSM) but its role is not to strengthen the market economy. On the contrary, just like the NAM, the INSM tries to teach us that more freedom for the companies is good for everyone. Even though they call their goal "market economy", the goal is in fact capitalism. There is still some truth in the saying: Never judge a book by its cover.

But the INSM wasn't the first lobby-organization in Germany. Right after the Second World War, the industry founded the "Bunderverband der Deutschen Industrie" (Federal association of the German industry, BDI) in 1949.

Its goal was also capitalism, and not a market economy as could clearly be seen in the 1950s. In these years, the Minister for Economic Affairs, Ludwig Erhard, tried to establish a law against monopolies. This would have been the first of its kind in Germany (monopolies have not been illegal in Germany before, unlike in the USA where they were declared illegal already at the end of the 19th century). And this law was heavily opposed by the industry and the BDI. The BDI even declared in the name of its members that the companies would stop all donations to the governing party if the law should pass. As this was an election year, the then-chancellor Konrad Adenauer stopped the voting of the law so his party would still get the donations. It seemed that the companies had achieved their goal with their open attempt of blackmailing.

But the blatant attempt of the companies to take control of the state wasn't successful for long: Right after the election and safely reinstalled in power, Adenauer let the parliament vote and the law entered into force.

Such an open clash of forces was unusual in the history of lobbying. Generally, the lobbyists work behind the curtain, in the dark, and the people will never know what really happened. You can imagine how powerful the lobby-groups are if you just look at their number. There are more than 15,000 lobby groups in Brussels and more than 2,100 in Germany (from only 1,500 15 years ago).

Today, you cannot be sure that the news you read in a newspaper or on the internet has really been written by a journalist or instead by a public relation agent working for a company. In many cases, newspapers and magazines are just copying the press-releases of companies and only give the impression that it is the work of a journalist (quite often even this "make-up" is done by the companies). There are roughly 20,000 PR-agents working in the USA – much more than actual journalists. What we read isn't quite often the news, but an advert coming in the shape of the news.

The federal government in Germany wanted to improve the collaboration between companies and the administration. Since 2004, there is the possibility for company employees to work in a ministry for some time and for a bureaucrat to work at a company. Maybe it is not surprising that this offer has been used generously by the companies, and mostly huge companies. The reason is that the "changeovers" are still paid by their original employer – they only work somewhere else. And a smaller company doesn't have the resources to pay additional employees.

So the program was mainly used by employees of several industry associations, Deutsche Telekom, IBM, BASF and other giants. And their time at the administration wasn't fruitless: Some of them could contribute to new laws. It were actual employees of the Deutsche Börse AG (German Stock Market, Inc.) and the Federal Association of Investment Groups that contributed to a law which finally legalized hedge-funds in Germany. And the head of company strategy of DaimlerChrysler was working at the Department of Transport when the Department had to decide which company should get the mandate to collect road charges for trucks on German highways. The mandate was finally given to TollCollect, a company in which DaimlerChrysler had huge stakes.

This seems to be quite a practical approach: Let the companies who know their business best write the laws that affect their business.

Why would we think that this is a bad thing? The companies are the rulers in the Western countries, anyway. The people still go to an election, but to be fair: An election where those really in power don't even run for office is nothing but a waste of time and seems to be nothing more than an entertaining event for the masses.

Those really in power simply are there, and will stay there.

Slave citizens

We have made it. We have realized the "free enterprise" concept in the Western world. But is this what we really wanted?

We may have governments, we may have elections, and we are supposed to be living in a democracy. But in fact the companies have a huge say in what's being done in our countries. Free enterprises can decide how they treat their incomes and where to tax it – with the results that they don't tax it at all. Free enterprises can decide how to produce their goods and what to tell us – with the result that they keep important information hidden from us. Free enterprises can influence the rules of the game as they control enormous amounts of money and the jobs we all depend on – with the results that they prefer those laws and those countries that favor their never ending appetite for higher gains. Free enterprises use their power to get richer; they don't care about the community they are living in.

Free enterprises are collecting incredible amounts of money. Apple had collected 137 billion dollars by the end of 2012. Microsoft has roughly 60 billion dollars on its accounts. On the same time, the average income of most employees (when considering inflation) has been stable since years or has even declined in the last twenty years. The companies are avoiding taxes, stealing it from the society, and making a lot of money, but not for the people working there. They do it for the people who own the companies – or at least believe it.

The thirty companies listed on the German DAX paid 28 billion Euros in dividends in 2013 to their shareholders. The total amount of money being handed over to investors just in Germany is uncountable. This is the money the companies made by selling their products to the consumers and stealing it from the society. Billions and billions of dollars are changing hands each year, moving from the poor to the rich. And this amount is increasing as the power of the companies over the state is increasing. We are at the mercy of big money.

Another huge part of money the huge companies are making by squeezing out the state is moving in the hands of those who believe they own the companies: The top management.

The income of some CEOs is simply unbelievable. Incomes of a few million dollars like the income of the CEO of Deutsche Bank with 9 million Euros seems to be high and unfair because it is some 400 times higher than the income of the worst paid employee at Deutsche Bank. But it is nothing compared to incomes of some American Managers. Angelo Mozilo of Countrywide Financial made 142 million dollars and Barry Doller of InterActiveCorp even made 295 million dollars in their best year. By the way: Countrywide Financial nearly went bankrupt during the financial crises and had to be saved by the Bank of America. It is now active under the name "America Home Loans". But be sure that Mozilo had its money in a save harbor by then.

However, even these incomes are peanuts compared to the ones some of most prominent hedge-fund managers were able to make. The most successful one has probably been John Paulson who earned 3.7 billion dollars in 2008. But that was mainly due to the bets he made against the Abacus-derivatives he helped to sell, so maybe it doesn't count as fairly earned income. The legendary George Soros, by the way, made only 2.9 billion that year. And in 2009, when the whole industry had crumbled and the GDPs of all major nations fell, the 23 most important financial institutes in the USA paid 140 billion dollars as bonuses to their employees – 10 billion more than in 2007, the year before the financial crisis. But to be fair: It needs really highly effective and hard-working employees to bring the whole world down. In former times this was done by ruthless dictators who had whole armies at their hands, and not by some greenhorns who had only shaven last week for their first time.

The wealth of the upper class is increasing at an incredible speed. In 1982 it needed 92 million dollars to make it on Forbes' Top-400-List of the wealthiest people. In 200 the minimum wealth was 725 million dollars.

That's the result of decades of "free enterprise" politics. Make sure the companies and those in power feel good, and the state will feel good. So the countries reduced the taxes, but mainly the top rates, from more than 70 percent to just below 40 percent in the USA and from 56 to 42 percent in Germany. We just described the effect: Even more money stayed in the hands of the rich, and now it takes more than 700 million dollars to make it on the list of the superrich.

On the other hand, the class of the poor is growing. More and more people are poor. The unemployment statistics may not look too bad, and in fact in Germany it looks better today than during the last 20 years, but in today's world you can even be poor while working hard. In fact, many people now have two or three jobs just to survive –

not to finance long vacations or extravagant hobbies. Those who can afford these luxuries don't have to work at all.

The number of poor people in rich countries is growing steadily. Many Americans lost their homes and are living in their cars. As Americans prefer SUVs, at least their new homes are not too small.

Many Germans are working even though they don't earn enough money for a decent living with their 40-hours-week. The reason is that Germany is about the only industrialized country without minimum wages. And so people sometimes earn less than four or even three Euros per hour. They don't have contracts that mention such low hourly wages. On the contrary, they have contracts that promise them much higher wages. But they don't get paid by the hour, they get paid for the amount of work they are doing. The companies are calculating typical times how long it might take to get the work done, but for some reasons they never get it right: In reality it takes much longer – and the hourly wages are decreasing and decreasing.

The growth of this "low-wage-segment", as it is called, didn't happen by chance. It was the open goal of the German government, of the first pure "left" government in Germany. One can assume that the "left" government wanted to prove to the real rulers of the country that they could make decent politics by betraying their own electorate.

This politics, however, helped to reduce the unemployment rate in Germany. It is now one of the lowest. Okay, the people working in the "low-wage-segment" (about one quarter of the German workforce) are really poor, and the low wages are eroding the wages of "normal" work, but the unemployment rate is low. And that seems to be all that matters.

Low wages (at least for the working population) seem to be the only right way to win in a globalized world. And Germany is taking this path without further ado. This is the secret of Germany's success in the times after the financial crisis. Every other country was still suffering from the economic blow, only Germany was taking the path to low wages and succeeded. Germany's slaughterhouses are only paying starvation wages, but are now the most successful ones in Europe. The wages are so low that even desperate Germans don't work there – hundreds of desperate people from Eastern European countries like Romania or Bulgaria are carried to the slaughterhouses to work there. After all, a Euro is still a lot of money there.

France was once the biggest producers of asparagus in Europe. But harvesting the asparagus is labor intensive. It is more expensive in countries with higher wages. France has minimum wages, Germany hasn't. Guess which country is today Europe's biggest producer of asparagus.

Some European companies used to produce everything in their home-country. But with a low-wage China just across the border, some steps of the production have been outsourced to Germany. Only some years ago, every step of the production was done in the home-country, now only some steps are done here, then the parts are transported to Germany, the next production steps are performed in Germany, and the parts go back to the home-country where the last production steps are performed. Germany's economy is so successful because it is preying on the economy of its neighbors.

Germans have always been good at following the rules. Today, the rules are not set by a dictator or a democratically elected government, today the rules are set by international companies. And they only know one rule: Make the production cheap.

Germany is doing its best to be the first in class.

But although Germans are best in class, this is happening all over the world. A minority of wealthy people, using the power of international companies that dwarfs the power of states, is dictating the rules. We believe that elections can change something, but we don't have the chance to elect the real rulers. They dictate the rules of the game, and if we don't want to obey, they threaten to move jobs abroad. Blackmailing has become the standard in politics.

Capitalism replaced the market economy, an oligarchy replaced democracy. The enterprises are free; the citizens are slaves to them.

Welcome to our world.

The Pressure is Rising

A small minority takes the power in its hands, a small minority profits from the laws in the Western countries, and only a small minority increases its wealth while the majority of the people only achieves to keep its wealth or even gets poorer. When there is only a small minority profiting from today's politics, how come that there is no general outcry, that there is not a general feeling of injustice and the need to change politics?

The reason might be that the majority doesn't believe or doesn't want to believe that they are on the losing side. Our society is roughly divided in two parts: the winners and the losers, the rich and the poor. Some say there is a large middle-class in between, but its size is shrinking, its power is dwindling. Now consider your own position in the society. You know that the chances are higher that you are part of the losing and poor majority. But would you agree that you are part of this majority? You might own a car, have a job, and you might even own a house. You are definitely not poor. You don't want to be part of the losing majority. So whenever laws are proposed that support the rich and are against the poor, you support these laws, because these laws are in *your* interest. You are part of the winning side; you are a member of the rich society. Poor dreamer.

But as long as the majority of the people think they are part of the rich side, as long as they refuse to believe that they are part of the losing side, no changes will occur. The mechanisms of democracy which are still in place will not be activated. A minority decides in which direction our society goes, and the majority doesn't oppose these decisions, although it will suffer from these decisions. As long as the majority silently agrees, the minority can continue.

But the pressure is rising. And there are signs that this will not continue forever. The most promising signs are coming from a country that has been known as the harbor of the rich – but also as the homeland of democracy: Switzerland.

The Swiss got tired of the ever increasing gap between the rich and the poor in their country. They no longer accept that the members of a managing board can earn so much more than the people working in the same company. So they have already decided that the stock-holders of Swiss companies have to decide about the income of the members of a managing board – and no longer the managers and their buddies from the governing body. This process only led to ever increasing incomes as friends will be friends – and when one manager agrees to a higher income of another, he also sets a higher standard for his income.

This decision was done in a referendum. And the Swiss even considered a next step: They want to set a limit for the income of the members of a managing board. Some of them didn't accept any longer that their incomes are several hundred times higher than the income of the poorest employees. In the case of Novartis, the income of the CEO was 720 times higher. These numbers cannot be justified – and they should never occur again. So some Swiss started the "Initiative 1:12", meaning that the maximum monthly income of a CEO should only be as high as the yearly income of the poorest employee. When the referendum was voted end of 2013, the initiative lost, but it showed that the resistance against greedy behavior of the elite is growing.

And there is more resistance to the power of companies. Funny enough, it's all happening in Europe. The companies seem to have already won the battle in the USA.

The two largest battle fields are genetically modified organisms and fracking. Both are not questioned in the USA and largely used although their side-effects are, to say the least, questionable.

The situation is completely different in Europe. Genetic engineering and fracking are considered very critically, and they are generally not used. Fracking is even banned in France. And Monsanto communicated in the summer of 2013 that it will not continue with its applications for a release of genetically modified plants in Europe. This might be a diversionary tactic as the US government is trying to establish genetically modified organisms in Europe through the talks about a free-trade zone between the European Union and the USA, but for the moment the companies have not achieved their goals.

The people of Europe oppose these dangerous technologies. They don't want genetically modified organisms when naturally bred organisms are sufficiently effective, and they don't want to use fracking when alternative energy sources are available.

The governments, however, are not always so straightforward. They haven't given up on gene-food and fracking. Which is not really a surprise as they are controlled by the companies; and they only see the money and not the risk. If a risk should manifest itself, it will be the state that's paying, anyway, it will be the tax payers, the poor, and not the rich. We saw the tactics during the financial crisis: Thousands of bankers earned billions of dollars, but when the economy went down the drain due to their acting, they didn't participate with even one dollar to solve the problems they had caused.

A democracy needs people to work. They have to raise their voice; otherwise the ruthless will take over. For what are the first words of the American constitution?

"We the people…"

The Deceived Middle Class

Times without a Middle Class

If we were asked to divide our society in classes, we would probably come up with three different classes (maybe after stating that there are no real classes in the sense that there are real boundaries between them that reduce the social mobility to zero – we will see later how true this statement is): The first would be the upper class, the superrich who don't have to worry about anything and seem to be swimming in money like the well-known duck Scrooge from Walt Disney. Then there is the lower class with those that don't have enough to live on, who are hungry, do not possess anything but rags and quite often don't even have a place to live (living under a bridge is not really a place you can call home). Both classes are very small in our today's society (I am talking about the industrialized countries). Only a minority is rich enough to live in absolute luxury, and only a minority is so poor that it doesn't know in the morning how it will survive the day.

The by far biggest class in our society is the middle class. The middle class is not so rich than it could easily by a Lamborghini, a yacht or a villa with twenty bedrooms and even more bathrooms (for whatever reason you might need them – maybe for the same reason that you buy a car that has a top speed of 280 km/h and will only be used on streets with a speed limit of 120 km/h). And it also is not so poor that it doesn't know today how it should survive tomorrow.

The people of the middle class are rich enough that they can buy the food they like without having to count every

Cent, they are rich enough that they have a car (may it be a small compact car or some luxury car), that they have a roof above their head (either a small apartment or a big house with a huge garden), and that they can offer themselves vacations at least once a year and generally abroad. The middle class is somewhere between the upper class and the lower class; its member are not really rich, but they have enough money to lead a decent life.

We are so used to having a middle class, because there are so many of us, that is might be a surprising fact to learn that the middle class as we know it today is a rather new invention. In fact, it's younger than the industrial revolution.

Our modern civilization was born about then thousand years ago in what we call today the "Middle East". It is here that we find the oldest traces of agriculture; signs that humans have managed to dominate nature and change it to his advantage by domesticating animals and plants. Some hundred years later, agriculture was also invented in China, independently from the people of the Middle East. And much, much later (about 5000 years ago) agriculture was established independently from the Eurasian sources in the Americas.

But the seeds that were grown in the Middle East were the source of the civilizations that spread around the Mediterranean Sea, reached the Egyptians, the Greeks, and finally the Romans. The culture that came with it, the philosophy, mathematics, and science was the basis of the European culture (although much of it got lost during the Dark Ages and had to be rediscovered with the help of the Arabs during the Renaissance). It was this culture that developed an industrial revolution, it was this culture that traveled around the world – and mainly conquered it, first by force, later on by its seducing culture (which, since the beginning of the 20th century, became more and more North American based).

Why the culture of the Middle East was finally the superior culture – if it was only due to the fact that it had a head start, or because it invented a culture that put the individual in its center – can be the source for a lot of speculations. The fact is simply that the Western culture, as we call the civilization that started in the Middle East today, is the dominating culture of our times.

But it is only since about a century that our society has its today's structure. Before that time, and since millennia, the Western society could simply be divided into two classes: The upper class, the priests and the aristocrats, and the lower class, the workers and the peasants. There was no in-between.

The upper class consisted of those members of the society who made the decisions. They concentrated all the power and wealth of the society in their hands. Quite often they justified the fact that they dominated the society by claiming that they were the direct descendants of the gods. But sometimes they just clung to their position by brute force. As they dominated the state and the army, they had all the power they needed to keep their position in case someone should question it.

The lower class collected the rest of the population, which was the overwhelming majority. In spite of its size, it didn't possess any rights or wealth whatsoever. The members of the lower class were completely at the mercy of the upper class. Their life was a daily struggle for survival. Sometimes, the lower class stood up and rebelled against their life-conditions. Sometimes, the lower class requested a fair share in power and the wealth of the society. But these rebellions didn't last long. In general, they were suppressed with force.

But not all rebellions were ended by force, some were ended by reason. That's at least the message we get from a story that supposedly happened in the 4th century B.C. in Rome. Like any other civilization so far (and like many others still to come) the Roman society was divided into two classes: The upper class and the plebs who did all the work while the upper class contented itself with making decisions and enjoying life.

One day, the plebs decided that they had enough. They didn't want to tolerate it any longer that the upper class led its lazy life and they had to do all the work – while receiving almost nothing for their hard work. So the plebs went on strike and moved to the holy mountain Mons Sacer.

This strike left the upper class in Rome with a problem: They were used to giving orders, but they didn't really know how things worked and were neither willing nor capable of doing the daily work themselves.

The upper class thus required that the strike should be ended quickly. But they didn't use force against the plebs (maybe there were far too many of them). Instead, they sent their consul Menenius Agrippa to talk to the plebs. And Menenius talked to the people. He didn't negotiate with them and tried to convince them to come back in exchange for some improvements. Instead, he told them an allegory:

There once was a time, he said, when all parts of the body had their own mind and their own will. But the limbs grew tired of doing all the work while the stomach was lying around lazily and not doing anything. So the limbs decided to go on strike: The hands would no longer bring food to the mouth, and the mouth would no longer chew it. Hunger, they thought, would be the best weapon to bring the stomach to its knees (figuratively speaking) and let him make concessions.

But they just had started with their strike when the whole body became weak. This made them understand that the stomach wasn't just lying around lazily, but that it also did valuable things for the good of all. Only together, limbs and stomach, they would be able to keep the body alive. Thus the limps stopped their rebellion and reconciled themselves with the stomach.

Every limp has its position in a body where it performs its task to make the body work. Similarly, every human being has his position in the society on which he has to perform his task. The plebs has to do their work as the limbs have to do theirs. And the upper class does the thinking just like the stomach – well, here the allegory has some weakness as the stomach is actually doing some work, only it's not moving around so we might assume it's also only thinking.

The message is: Things are as they are, and they cannot be changed. Everybody has to fulfill his duty, even if he doesn't like it (this request is of course easier if you are lying on a satin bed).

This understanding, that the two classes had to do their work and there was no way it could be changed, was shared during the Middle Ages in Europe. At this time, the society consisted of two classes: The priests and the aristocrats, who formed the upper class, did all the thinking, talking and preaching, and the peasants who formed the lower class that did all the hard work.

The society of the Middle Ages (at least the upper class) referred to the Bible to justify this division of the society in two classes:

According to the Bible, there once was a time when Noah got really drunk. His son Ham was expected to ignore his behavior or even cover it up. Instead, he made publicly fun of his drunken father. This enraged Noah who cursed Ham and all of his descendants to be the servants of all other men. And the descendants of Ham were the peasants, it's as simple as that.

So even if the upper class wanted to alleviate the fate of the lower class, they couldn't. If they did, they would be acting against the Bible, so everything had to stay as it was – and it was good the way it was.

Times moved on, the Middle Ages made place to the renaissance, the re-birth of Greek science and philosophy which were lost during the time Christianity dominated Europe, and finally the improved understanding of mechanics led to the greatest turmoil in human history: The industrial revolution.

The industrial revolution changed the look of the world. Long iron trails crossed the countries, and huge, steaming machines were moving along them from city to city. Whole quarters of cities transformed into huge factories that produced large amounts of coal and steel. And a 324 meter high tower made of steel became the new monument of Paris.

But even though the industrial revolution changed the look of the world, it didn't change the structure of society. Society still was divided into an upper and a lower class. If at all, the industrial revolution made the situation even worse for the members of the lower class.

Up to the industrial revolution, the lower class had been working on the country side. They were not rich, they could hardly survive, but they were farming their own plants, their family and friends were close by and they had at least some control over their life. But the ever increasing population made millions of them move into the city, looking for jobs, looking for a better life. But all they found was a desperate situation where they were at the mercy of the upper class.

The industrial revolution with its factories and new products needed many workers. But the growing population in Europe provided even more workers than the factories could employ. Millions of workers were looking for jobs, willing to take any chance to work. The capitalists knew this – and they played the game to their advantage. They were the masters of the jobs and thus the masters of the workers. They could decide under which conditions the workers should work, how many hours and for how much money. If workers didn't agree to these conditions – well, there were others waiting just outside the door to make this miserable job.

The working and living conditions of the poor were indescribable. They were working long hours, since their early youth, every day of the week. When they came of age, their bodies were nothing but ruins, unable to work any longer.

Whole families of eight or ten members were living in one room. The sanitary conditions were worse than anything the people of the Middle Ages had experienced. The food was rotten and the cloths were rags, and that was all they possessed. Animals in the palaces of the rich had a better life than the workers in the ever growing cities of the industrial revolution.

The desperate situation of the lower class even alarmed the Catholic Church that didn't have a problem with the also unjust but less severe situation during the Middle Ages. Pope Leo XIII had to remind the rich that they shouldn't treat their workers like slaves. But for once that the church was on the side of the poor, the rich didn't pay attention. The life of slaves in ancient times had been better than the life of workers during the industrial revolution. After all, you had to pay to own a slave, but you could get a worker for free. So their life wasn't worth a dime.

The workers were hardly able to survive with the money they earned in the factories. If they were sick for a day, they didn't earn money, and this meant they had to live without food that day. There was no insurance against the hardship of life. And nobody saw the necessity to increase the wages of the workers, on the contrary. The "iron law of wages", as it was called by the economist David Ricardo, clearly stated that the workers should only get so much money that they were able to survive, not one Cent more.

If they got more money, so the argument went, they would have more children, so there would be more workers on the market. The demand for workers, however, wouldn't increase only because there were more poor people living in the cities (the industrial revolution at that time was mainly consisting of heavy industry, building railways and ships for the state). With a higher supply of workers but a stable demand, this would mean that the wages of the workers would decrease according to the law of demand-and-supply. In the end, nothing would have changed; the workers would get the low wages they get today. So why bother giving the workers higher wages in the first place?

And if the workers tried to unit, if the workers went on strike and tried to force the capitalists to improve their life-conditions, their protest was suppressed immediately. The state issued rules forbidding the workers to form unions or negotiate their wages collectively. And if they didn't follow the rules, if they didn't follow the orders given by the capitalists, the stated unleashed its police and taught the workers how they should behave.

Before the 19th century, the state didn't see a problem to fight the workers and support the upper class. At that time – as for millennia before – the state was an institution of and for the upper class. Some countries might have called themselves a democracy already in the 18th or 19th century, but this was a democracy for an elite, just as the Greek democracy only existed for the men of the upper class (and not even the women of the upper class).

Also Prussia claimed to be a democracy in the 19th century. Officially, the whole male population was allowed to vote. But the votes were divided into three groups, each of them had one third of the votes: The first group consisted of the richest voters who paid the upper third of the taxes. The second group consists of the second richest voters who paid the second third of the taxes. And the third group consisted of all the men who paid the last third of the taxes. In many communities, the first and second group consisted of just one man each, so that two men had two thirds of all votes. Prussia could claim to have democratic elections, but as the rule wasn't "one man, one vote", it didn't really matter what the majority wanted.

All this only changed by the end of 19th century and the society was forced from two sides to make this change. It was a push-and-pull-change.

The Rise of the Middle Class

The push that led to the change was the push exercised by the workers who got tired with their conditions of living. The workers wanted a change – and they did everything they could to realize the change. They realized that they were a power simply by the enormous mass they represented. So they formed unions and founded political parties. The push that led to changes was the socialist and communist movement.

The pull that led to the changes came from an unexpected side: The upper class (at least some of them) realized that they actually needed the workers, as the situation had changed. Suddenly the upper class needed a mass of people with decent income to get the economy going, because the economy had changed to a consumer economy.

But let's start with the push-side of the story. The situation of the workers during the industrial revolution was desperate. Life wasn't easy in their villages, but at least they had some land they could grew vegetables on and they had their family and friends whom they had known since their birth and who could help them during tough times. But in the big cities, far away from their home, they were left to themselves. There were thousands of them, but nevertheless they were alone, the working traditions and social structures of the villages were no longer available in the cities. They were uprooted and had to find a new community.

At the same time, their conditions of living were unsupportable. They were eating, sleeping and mainly working; their life consisted of nothing else. They didn't seem to be humans, but machines made of flesh. They couldn't stand this situation much longer. Something had to change.

And as there were so many of them who shared this desperate life, they occasionally found together spontaneously to demonstrate against their conditions of living, to go on strike to improve their life. But these first signs of a rebellion were quickly dealt with by the state. The police was used to show the workers their limits and to arrest those who seemed to be the cause for the unrest. Quickly, everything went back to normal, and nothing had changed.

The situation only improved, when the workers started to institutionalize their protest, when they formed unions and political parties whose job it was to organize the protest against the conditions of living of the workers.

One important landmark in this context was the work of Karl Marx who provided a deeper understanding of the workers' situation and thus helped to generate a joint identity for all workers.

Marx described the situation of the workers with the one word: Exploitation. The workers were exploited by the capitalists. That's what the problem was.

The capitalist was paying the workers for a few hours of work, but in fact they were working much longer. This added value was the money that went into the pockets of the capitalists – and it was stolen from the workers.

Marx was convinced that the workers would not tolerate this unfair treatment of the capitalists for much longer, that there would be a workers' revolution that would turn the class system upside down and finally lead to a classless society.

Karl Marx and Friedrich Engels published the basic ideas of the workers' situation in their famous "Communist Manifesto" (where they say that the division of the society into two classes is a new phenomenon – although it was the standard during all of human civilization and only became more pronounced during the industrial revolution):

> "The history of all hitherto existing society is the history of class struggles.
>
> Freeman and slave, patrician and plebeian, lord and serf, guild-master and journeyman, in a word, oppressor and oppressed, stood in constant opposition to one another, carried on an uninterrupted, now hidden, now open fight, a fight that each time ended, either in a revolutionary reconstitution of society at large, or in the common ruin of the contending classes.

In the earlier epochs of history, we find almost everywhere a complicated arrangement of society into various orders, a manifold gradation of social rank. In ancient Rome we have patricians, knights, plebeians, slaves; in the Middle Ages, feudal lords, vassals, guild-masters, journeymen, apprentices, serfs; in almost all of these classes, again, subordinate gradations.

The modern bourgeois society that has sprouted from the ruins of feudal society has not done away with class antagonisms. It has but established new classes, new conditions of oppression, new forms of struggle in place of the old ones.

Our epoch, the epoch of the bourgeoisie, possesses, however, this distinct feature: it has simplified class antagonisms. Society as a whole is more and more splitting up into two great hostile camps, into two great classes directly facing each other — Bourgeoisie and Proletariat."

This existing order has to be overcome by the workers. There will be a communist revolution.

"In short, the Communists everywhere support every revolutionary movement against the existing social and political order of things.

...

The Communists disdain to conceal their views and aims. They openly declare that their ends can be attained only by the forcible overthrow of all existing social conditions. Let the ruling classes tremble at

a Communistic revolution. The proletarians
have nothing to lose but their chains. They
have a world to win."

And the Manifesto ended with the famous appeal:

"Working Men of All Countries, Unite! "

It was the open goal of the communist movement to turn
the society upside-down; they wanted to make a revolution.
The socialist movement generally didn't go that far, it
wanted to change society without overthrowing it; they
wanted to have an evolution which led to more rights for
the workers. For the upper class these fine differences
didn't really matter, as they would lose power in both cases.
So they opposed the labor movement wherever they could.
And when we talk of upper class, this means state and
government in these times.

As the labor movement gained momentum, the state
gathered all its forces to fight back. In a first step, the labor
movements like unions or political parties were declared
illegal. You couldn't publish anything in favor of the labor
movement; you couldn't house a meeting in favor of the
labor movement. Any activity that helped the workers
would put you at risk of being thrown into jail.
Nevertheless, the labor movement lived on in hiding.

As you couldn't put the majority of the population in jail,
the government had to find another way to fight the labor
movement. The fact that made these movements so
popular was that they provided a basic social security for its
members. When you were ill, you were not left on your
own and could see how you survived without money
(because you didn't get any money if you didn't work, in
contrast to the upper class who had so much wealth that
they didn't have to work at all and lived in a constant social
net). The state didn't provide any support for the poor in

tough times, only the labor movement provided such a support.

The German chancellor Otto von Bismarck thought he could lure away workers from the labor movement if he (i.e. the state) provided some social security for the workers, if he showed them that the state cared and was on their side. So he created a health insurance system in Germany (the first step into social security). And in addition, he it mandatory for all workers, so that they wouldn't have much money left for the voluntary membership in the labor movement. This, so Bismarck hoped, would weaken the labor movement and appease the situation.

Unfortunately, this didn't work out. Although the labor movement was forbidden and Bismarck tried to lure the workers away from it, it grew stronger and stronger. Independent representatives, who were nevertheless known to be close to the labor movement, received more and more votes during the elections. If the social democrats had been a legal party during this time, they would have been the biggest political group in the German parliament.

The pressure grew on politics to accept the labor movement as a legitimate political movement and by the end of the 19th century the labor movement was finally accepted as a legal political power. The state had understood that it couldn't win the battle against the workers (after all, the majority of the population) – so it stopped it. And since then, the state was no longer the state it used to be.

Up to the end of the 19th century, the stated used to be an institution of the upper class for the upper class, meant to stabilize the power of the upper class over the rest of the population. But with the workers gaining more and more power, the state changed. Step by step it understood itself as the caretaker for all people in the state, the rich and the poor alike. For the first time in history, real democratic societies emerged that included the whole population, the rich and the poor, male and female.

As the government now depended on the support of the whole population, and as the workers provided the majority of the votes, the government started to take care of their needs. Several laws concerning the job safety, working hours and wages were enacted. The workers finally had these rights in the society that the upper class had refused to grant them for millennia.

One might observe, that the governments in Europe already decided some laws concerning job safety at the beginning of the 19th century, well before the labor movement became a strong political power. These laws mainly concerned child labor. Many governments like those in England and Prussia enacted some laws against child-work. The laws in England, for instance, forbade the work of children under 9 years and limited to working hours to 48 hours per week for children between nine and thirteen years and 69 hours per week for children between fourteen and eighteen years. These working hours look still barbaric from today's view. And the reason to enact them was not even humanitarian:

The government had simply found out that workers, who had been working long hours during their early childhood, were so weak and crippled when adults that they could no longer be used as soldiers in the army. But the army needed a fresh supply of soldiers (as cannon fodder), so the government had to assure this supply. And if long working hours in an early childhood were the problem, then long working hours during childhood were forbidden – and the workers could come to age mainly unharmed so they could serve their time in the army.

*

The push side, the threat of a workers' revolution was only one factor that helped to improve the situation of the workers. There was also a pull side: Suddenly the workers were needed – but only if they earned more than the minimum amount they needed to barely survive, only if they earned more than dictated by the iron law of wages.

The cause for this change of mind was a changing economy. Up to the end of the 19th century, the economy was dominated by the heavy industry. Coal and steel were the raw materials that fed the economy. Endless railway tracks covered the landscape, steam and smog polluted the air, and machines seemed to be everywhere. Mechanics and thermodynamics were the subjects in physics that you had to learn if you wanted to make your career as an engineer in the industrial revolution.

All this changed during the 19th century, as a new physical force came to the attention of the scientists and engineers: Electricity.

Electricity wasn't really a completely new force. The ancient Greek already knew about electricity. They knew that e.g. amber behaved strangely when you rubbed it with a piece of cloth: It got "charged" and attracted small pieces of e.g. paper. Our name for the negative electric charge, the electron, is derived from the Greek word for amber.

But this kind of electricity was only static. You had some kind of force that attracted things, but there was nothing else you could do with it, so it remained a curiosity throughout the following centuries up to the 18th century.

It was only when the industrial revolution was already on its way that scientists looked again at this strange phenomenon of static electricity. It was the right time: Science had become quite popular in Europe; any new phenomenon could attract the attention of the public. And many rich men entertained their guests with scientific experiments in the evening (remember: This was well before the time the TV was invented).

Electricity proved to be a nice subject to entertain the public. Just think of the experiments you could do with a strong static electric field as it is produced by a van der Graaf generator. If you touch the metallic sphere that collects the charges, your hair will stand on end as if it tries to escape from your head. This doesn't only make children laugh.

Apart from entertaining their guests, the scientists of the 18th and 19th century made several experiments to see what else could be done with electricity. In the course of their experiments they understood that electric and magnetic fields interacted, they understood that electricity didn't have to be static but could flow from one side to another, and they even showed that electromagnetic waves could be transmitted through empty space.

It was only a question of time that the first electric generators (to create electricity from e.g. steam) and first electric motors (to move machines) were available. And it took only about a century after the first deeper investigations into the phenomenon of electricity had started up to the point that the English physicist James Clerk Maxwell wrote down four easy equations that described the whole variety of electric and magnetic phenomena – and even predicted that light is some kind of electromagnetic wave.

With the physics behind electricity understood and the possibility to generate it wherever you wanted, hundreds of inventors thought how they could use this new force. The best known of these inventors is probably the American inventor Thomas Alva Edison. His most famous invention is the light bulb, although he wasn't the first the use an electric current to heat a metal wire so it would start to emit light; he was only the most successful. And in addition, he came up with the screw thread that made it easy to replace broken light bulbs. That's why incandescent light bulbs are often called Edison bulbs in English-speaking countries.

But the light bulb wasn't his only invention. With the money of his first inventions, he built a laboratory in Menlo Park, New Jersey, where he and his team professionally worked on inventions. It worked like the research group of modern companies, always trying to come up with new products that could make money. Some the inventions that made it from Menlo Park into the world were the phonograph and a microphone. In addition, Edison spent some time to establish the electricity network for New York, the first of its kind in the world.

And due to the technology Edison used it would also remain the last of its kind. Edison preferred direct current to alternating current, because direct current is less dangerous for humans than alternating currents. It has one big disadvantage, though: It is difficult to transform direct current from one voltage to another. If your generator is close to the machine that uses the electricity, there is no need to transform the voltages. But if your generator is in a big power plant outside the city, you might want to transform the voltage to higher voltages, because the resistance and thus the power loss are significantly lower at higher voltages.

Alternating current was thus promoted by the Czech inventor Nikola Tesla and his investor George Westinghouse. They showed that they could build huge power plants and transport the electricity over large distances with only a minimum loss, something Edison couldn't do with direct current (in his time, today we have some smart solutions to transform voltages even for direct current). But Edison was stubborn and pointed to the dangers of alternating current. To stress his point, he made another famous invention: The electric chair.

He used the electric chair on cats and horses to show how dangerous alternating current could be. But the investors wouldn't listen. As alternating current could be transported easily over large distances, it became the basis for our electricity nets – and the justice system used the electric chair to execute criminals.

Edison had probably never intended that one of his inventions should do harm. He only wanted to stress his point that alternating currents at high voltages are very dangerous. But history has its own sense of irony.

Electricity wasn't the only new energy source that was developed in the 19th century. The other one was oil.

Oil, or petroleum, has also been known since ancient times, and just like electricity it was not used widely. On the contrary: Some salt deposits also contained oil, but as nobody knew what to do with it, they were abandoned once the salt was too much contaminated by the oil.

If you needed oil to light a light, you used a resource that provided clean oil (not that dirty, black "rock oil" which is the literal translation for petroleum) and was available in abundance: Oil made from whale fat.

Whales were at least widely available as long as human kind hadn't figure out how to hunt them efficiently. In the 19th century, the number of whales decreased drastically while the demand of oil due to the growing population increased. So people were looking for another source of oil and turned again to petroleum.

But petroleum wasn't easily accessible. It was hidden well beneath the soil, and the problem was how to get it out of there. It was Edwin L. Drake who proposed a solution: He would drill for it. At first, he was sponsored by a company, but the success didn't materialized. He was living on his savings, when he finally succeeded: In the year 1859 in Titusville, Pennsylvania, he managed to tap into an oil field and produce 4000 liters of oil per day. Some years later, thousands of holes were drilled into the soil to extract the oil.

It was thanks to the now large availability of oil that another invention made sense: The combustion engine and finally the car.

The first car was invented by Carl Benz who filed his patent in 1885. It became famous when his wife Bertha took their two sons and made the first "long-distance" travel by car in 1888. They rode from Mannheim to Pforzheim and covered 104 km. The distance doesn't seem to be impressive today, but it was quite a distance in times when most of the people were travelling on foot.

The ride was very slow (it needed more than 12 hours to cover the distance), but progress couldn't be stopped. Today, the car is the symbol of our times, and you can cover the distance between Mannheim and Pforzheim in just two hours (if there is only the regular traffic jam).

*

Coal was the energy source of the first industrial revolution, electricity and oil became the energy sources for the second industrial revolution. These energy sources allowed for the production of much smaller and much more mobile products. They allowed for the production of consumer goods. The industry was thus moving from being dominated by the heavy industry to being dominated by the consumer industry. But this change was not only a change in the products. It also required a significant change with the regards to the customer base.

The customers of the first industrial revolution were mainly big companies and the state. The heavy industry provided investment goods that could only be bought by large institutions. The second industrial revolution, on the contrary, provided consumer goods that needed to be bought by individuals.

The only individual that had the money to buy the consumer goods, however, were the rich of the upper class. The members of the lower class only earned what they needed to survive, in line with the iron law of wages. The rich had even more money than they could spend on the consumer goods, but they provided only a very small customer base. In fact, the customer base was too small to make the second industrial revolution successful.

More than products, the second industrial revolution based on consumer goods needed consumers, it needed customers. The society somehow had to provide these customers, and there was only one way to go: Enable the lower class to become customers, which meant that the workers should earn more than the minimum they needed to survive. The consumer economy needed a large middle class to be successful.

One of the first entrepreneurs who understood this requirement was Henry Ford. Henry Ford is mainly known for his obsession to reduce the production costs of cars. He had spent his whole life figuring out where to save just another Cent. He even introduced the assembly line and reduced the work of his workers to a handful of movements (so that they worked like robots made from flesh) to reduce the costs. And he is quoted of having said that his customers could chose any color for their car that they wanted – provided it was black.

The reason was not that he could get this color cheaper than any other color. The reason was that black color dries faster than any other color. With measures like this Ford was able to reduce the production costs for a Ford model T from 825 dollars in 1908 to 360 dollars in 1916.

In the year 1913, Henry Ford made a decision that seemed mad at first glance: although he had been trying to reduce the production costs of his cars obsessively, he increased the wages of his workers to five dollars a days – which was twice the average income of workers at that time. Some economists pretend that the reason for this decision was to convince the workers to stay in his factories. His factories were not really popular with workers due to the stupid work at the assembly line. But there was more behind it. Ford had understood that the consumer economy needed consumers. If he wanted to sell his cars in large numbers, he needed consumers in large numbers. In the end, this meant that he had to pay them more than what they just needed to survive.

This is what Henry Ford meant when he wrote in this autobiography that

> "The scale of their [the workers'] living—
> the rate of their wages—determines the
> prosperity of the country."

A country can only be rich and prosper when all people earn enough to participate in the consumer capitalism. The wages of the workers are costs for the companies, but they are income for the society – and thus in the end also for the companies. If a company tries to reduce the costs by reducing the income of the company, then it will bite the hand that feeds it. If the workers don't have money to buy things, a company will not be able to sell things – and it will go bankrupt.

Many managers didn't understand this. They thought Ford had gone mad. And still today some managers refuse to understand this simple rule. In a sense, they are right. If only one company tries to maximize its profits by reducing its wages to an absolute minimum, it might get away with it. But if more and more companies are taking this way, if in the end the majority of the companies is acting like this, then the society will be damaged – and this includes the companies. No one will be the winner when wages are reduced on a large scale. That's why minimum wages are so important.

Even though managers didn't want to understand the importance of fair and high wages, the politicians did. They did this because the public told them so (after all, the workers now had the majority of votes in the democracies). But some politicians understood this for simple economic reasons. They really understood that a country could only prosper if it had a large consuming middle class, if it manages to lift as many people as it could from the lower class to the middle class.

One of the prominent examples is the former German Federal Minister for Economic Affairs, Ludwig Erhard, also known as the "father of the economic miracle" that boosted German economy after the Second World War. In his book "Wealth for All" he described the goals of his politics:

It is necessary

> "that every economic progress and each improvement in operation methods does not lead to higher gains, annuities or sinecures, but that all of these successes are passed on to the *consumer*. This is the *social* meaning of *market economy* that *each economic success* wherever it happens, that each advantage from rationalization, each improvement of operation methods is *made available to the well-being of the whole people*."

No politician would have made such a statement in the 19th century or before, but in the 20th century it was the common understanding of politicians and economists in the industrialized world that the workers should have their share in the growing wealth of the countries. More and more people joined the middle class, were able to buy or rent a decent apartment, buy a car and go on vacation at least once a year; the member of the middle class did what they had to do: They consumed to keep the economy running.

The lower class was almost forgotten. Some shattered souls, those who, for some reason, had lost any contact to society remained in the lower class. But even they could get some support from the state and social security so that their living conditions could be much better than they used to be during all the millennia before.

The push of the social movements that brought workers' parties into parliaments and assured a fair part of the power in the state for the workers, and the pull of the economy which needed an army of consumers assured that a huge middle class was formed for the first time in history in the industrialized countries.

But the rise of the middle class happened quickly. And the middle class can just as quickly disappear.

Threats to the Middle Class

The new class appeared because its members were no longer part of the lower class thanks to their moderate wealth. But on the other hand, they never made it to the upper class as well. There might have been some exceptions when someone could move from the lower class to the upper class, but this "from rags to riches"-stories only happened very rarely. The upper class is a closed society whose members only mingle very rarely with those that have been natural servant for millennia. It is like someone from the aristocracy marrying a commoner. It might happen, but it is not the norm.

This strict separation of classes – on the one side the upper class, on the other side the middle and lower class – is also the case in the United States, although you would assume that this new formed country that never possessed a classical aristocracy would have a much higher social mobility than European countries. And in fact there are examples that people make it to the superrich. But they generally started from the rich – and not from rags. The upper class stays among itself, even more so, as the education in the USA is mostly private, which means you can only participate if your parents are rich enough. If you don't have money, you won't get access. This barrier is significantly lower in Europe with its public higher education, and thus the social mobility in Europe is higher than in the USA.

But the lower class didn't mind. They weren't looking for a chance to become superrich. They were quite happy with having a decent income, i.e. with becoming a member of the middle class.

And the upper class didn't oppose the development as long as they would profit from it. As the consumer economy after the Second World War grew with unprecedented speed, the upper class became richer even though it had to share some of the additional wealth with the lower class. The companies paid higher wages, and yet the rich became richer. It was the classical win-win-situation.

But it is a platitude that every boom has to end, although we can't believe it as long as everything is going well. Our planet as a finite size, so everything that grows on it, and even if it is a whole economy, can only have a finite size. The ending of a boom always comes as a surprise to us, nevertheless it happens. In the case of the phenomenal economic growth of the consumer capitalism, the end appeared around the year 1970 in the industrialized world.

Some people blame the end of the miraculous growth to the oil crisis. Due to some quarrels about the existence of Israel, the Arab oil cartel OPEC reduced the production quota which led to a drastic increase of the oil price (even though it was only fractions of what we have to pay today). As the worldwide economy depended on oil, an increased oil price meant increased production costs for practically everything, this in turn reduced the demand – and the world moved into a recession.

This, at least, is the story that's been told. But the fact is that the economic growth had already ended at the end of the 1960s in major countries like the USA and Germany and that these countries had even experienced small recessions at that time. This was well before the Arab countries reduced the production quota.

The real reason for the end of the boom was simply a saturation of the markets. When the fridge, the electric stove, the radio and the television were invented at the beginning of the 20th century, nobody possessed such a good. And at first, there were not many people who could buy these goods as they were expensive. But then the prices declined, the lower class turned into a middle class, and suddenly millions of people could afford these new technical gimmicks. The whole nation was the market and the economy boomed. Companies were sometimes even unable to deliver the goods because the demand was so much higher than the supply.

But as everyone owned a fridge or television, the demand declined. Now, only broken goods were replaced by new ones, the market got saturated and the times were over that you found empty shelves in the store because your product was sold out and could only be delivered in a few weeks.

The real problem was that this did not only happen for fridges and televisions, but also for the electric stove, radios and cars. The demand for all these goods, for all the goods that characterized the second industrial revolution, became saturated around the year 1970. It was not just one market that became saturated, but the whole economy – and the boom was over. The oil crisis only made the end of the boom worse, but it didn't cause it.

In a saturated market, however the structure of the industrial production has to change. As long as the market is growing, as long as the demand is bigger than the supply, you don't really care about the production costs. The consumers will pay any price; they are eagerly waiting to receive their product, so why should you bother to make your product some percent cheaper? In theory, you might gain a bigger market share. But in the time of the boom the production is limited by the production capacity and not by the demand, so you won't be able to profit from it, anyway. That's why prices are higher when the market is growing, and that's also why companies don't care much about production costs in a booming market (at least it is not their number one priority).

That changes drastically in a saturated market. Now you can only grow if your competitors loose market shares. That means you have to be better than the competitors, which in most cases translates into: You have to be cheaper. Now the production costs are in the focus of your attention because they are your weapon against the competition.

Big cost positions in most companies are the personnel costs. After all, they had been growing significantly in the last years. As it is also easier to fire people and thus reduce the production costs, it is the obvious approach and taken by all companies to reduce production costs. As a consequence, the unemployment rate is rising.

According to simple economic rules, the costs for a good should decline if the demand declines. The cost for work, however, is fixed; no worker will agree to work for less. It is "inelastic" as the economists say. All you can do is to keep the wages stable, which will lead to a reduction of the cost over time due to inflation. This is a slow process to fix the unemployment rate, and a process where the middle class will lose money because they will earn less, inflation adjusted.

But this is exactly one of the solutions that was taken in the industrialized countries. The employees are making less money today if you consider inflation than they made some twenty years ago. The price for work decreased. But using inflation to decrease the price for work is a slow process. And the competition isn't sleeping.

To make things even worse: The competition after 1970 didn't only come from other industrialized countries facing the same problem. The competition came from emerging countries like China (with Japan starting some years earlier) that had a completely different social structure. In fact, their social system was a copy of the European social system of the first industrial revolution. This simply means, it didn't exist – and so these companies were able to produce their goods much cheaper at a comparable quality.

The emerging countries could profit from several reforms the international community had decided on in the 1970s and 1980s. These reforms led to a reduction of customs duties and finally to the inauguration of the World Trade

Organization (WTO) in 1994. The goal of these reforms was to ensure free trade between all countries.

It might seem counter-productive to ensure free trade between countries if this means a higher influx of goods from emerging markets into the industrialized countries which even makes the situation worse for the workers there. But politics was convinced it would be a good thing to reduce the trade barriers between the countries. They took the argument from David Ricardo.

David Ricardo was a British economist, one of the first who really devoted himself fully to economy and was thus called an economist (Adam Smith was just a philosopher who happened to write a book about economy). Ricardo was convinced that foreign trade would be to the advantage for all partners. He based his idea on something that he called "comparative advantage".

Ricardo was convinced that it isn't the absolute production cost that determines if foreign trade between two countries is advantageous for the two countries, but only the relative costs of production.

He explained this with cloth and wine production in England and Portugal. In both cases, the production costs were much lower in Portugal than in England. If the production of a certain amount of cloth required the costs of 100 man years in England, it only required 90 man years in Portugal. The difference is even bigger in the case of wine: As the climate is more favorable for wine production in Portugal than it is in England, the production of the same amount of wine requires only 80 man years in Portugal, but 120 man years in England.

If you only look at the relative costs, you would say that everything should be produced in Portugal and nothing in England, as both products can be produced much cheaper in Portugal. But Ricardo observed that it would be even more favorable for Portugal to focus its production on wine and stop the production of cloth. In this case, it could earn even more money, as the relative costs for wine are lower than for the production of cloth. With the same invest, it can thus produce more wine than cloth and make more money.

Following the same argument, England should concentrate on the production of cloth and stop the production of wine as the relative costs for the production of cloth are lower.

If each country focused on the products where it had a comparative advantage, both countries would profit and foreign trade would be to the benefit of all.

With this theory in mind, the nations set out to increase foreign trade by reducing the barriers between the countries. The problem with this theory is: It only works if all countries focus on the products where they have a comparative advantage. As soon as one country focuses on the products where it has an absolute advantage (as this is done at the moment in the emerging countries) then the nice theory disappears and leaves only ruins.

This is what happened in the globalized world. The nations didn't just look at the comparative advantage; they were looking at the absolute advantage. And the consequences weren't difficult to see: The workers of the rich countries entered in direct competition to the workers of the emerging countries – and the workers of the emerging countries had the huge advantage of lower wages.

To fight this even tougher competition, the companies of the industrialized countries had only one chance: They had to fight the competition with its own weapons. If the products of the companies of the industrialized countries should remain competitive, they had to be produced in the emerging countries as well. Therefore, the companies of the industrialized countries moved their production to the emerging countries and only shipped them home for consumption.

Thanks to new technologies like container ships, transporting the goods from one end of the world to another is very cheap today. So even though goods are produced in China and have to be shipped around half the world, they are still cheaper than goods that have been produced in Europe or the USA.

The globalized world in stagnating markets puts additional pressure on the middle class. The unemployment rate grew even higher, as the people at home were only needed for consumption but no longer for production.

How the economy should work if the middle class was meant to consume without receiving the means for consumption, is a mystery. But this wasn't the real problem seen in the estimation of the upper class. The real problem was that the higher competition due to the stagnating economy meant lower profits for the companies and thus for the upper class who owned these companies.

The upper class didn't mind sharing its profits with the lower class to create a middle class as long as the profits were rising. But now, with declining profits, the situation had changed. Sharing the wealth with the lower (middle) class would mean a decline in wealth for the upper class. And if there is one thing no human being likes – independent of the class he is part of – then it is losing money. Sharing money as long as you get richer is okay. Sharing money and getting poorer is out of the questions.

So the upper class was reconsidering the "social contract".

The End of the Middle Class

One important aspect in the history of economics is the role of the state in the national economy which has changed significantly over the last centuries. During the Renaissance, the European countries were governed by absolute monarchs, the most famous one is probably Louis XIV who could claim without any exaggeration: "L'état, c'est moi" (I am the state).

Like the absolute monarchs of the other countries, Louis XIV concentrated all the power in the state in his hands. He controlled the army, the police, and justice; simply everything. This also included the economy, after all this is the part of the state where the wealth is actually generated.

The economy system of the absolute monarchs was called mercantilism, and the economists of that time were mainly in favor of mercantilism. Maybe they didn't really have a choice: Mercantilism was meant to increase the power of the country, thus you could be considered unpatriotic, a traitor even, if you didn't support mercantilism.

The idea of mercantilism was easy: The state wanted to collect all the gold in the world (or as much of it as it could) and thus become the most powerful state in the world. To achieve this goal, the mercantilist states aggressively sold their goods abroad while at the same time increasing the customs duties to prevent other countries from selling their goods at home.

This is maybe a good idea to increase your economic power if you are the only one who acts like this. Unfortunately, all other states acted exactly like this as well, so the foreign trade practically stopped and no-one could win from it. All that was left from mercantilism was a state who told the factories and merchants what to do because he thought he knew best.

This changed after Adam Smith had published his celebrated "The Wealth of Nations" in 1776 (by coincidence the same year that the USA became independent from Great Britain – but Smith was a Scotsman and probably didn't care).

In this book Smith promoted a liberal economy that was no longer controlled by the state. The protagonists of the economy, the producers, merchants and consumers, should be free to choose what to produce and at what price to sell it. The state should content itself in providing the infrastructure like streets and harbors, but also the schools and the legal framework. He should, however, not actively interfere in the economy.

Some critics believed that selfish people would take control of the economy and dictate the rules, if the state abstained from interfering actively. But Smith stressed that he exactly trusted the people to be selfish:

> "It is not from the benevolence of the butcher, the brewer, or the baker that we expect our dinner, but from their regard to their own interest."

People have to act in self-interest to improve the situation. If they wouldn't see how they could improve their situation, nothing would advance. But this doesn't necessarily mean that only the selfish would profit from a liberal economy and the moral people would suffer, because there is Smith's famous invisible hand.

> "The rich...are led by an invisible hand to make nearly the same distribution of the necessaries of life, which would have been made, had the earth been divided into equal portions among all its inhabitants, and thus without intending it, without knowing it, advance the interest of the society."

Just let the rich do as they want, and everything will turn out fine, as long as the state doesn't interfere. After centuries of a state-dominated economy and society, this statement was strongly supported by the intellectuals of Smith's time. It fit into the framework of general freedom that was discuss by philosophers and politicians at his time and which lead to more democracy and human rights and less paternalism by the state.

Everything seemed fine – until that fateful day in 1929. On the so-called "Black Thursday", October 24th, the stock market in the USA crashed, taking with it the American economy and thus, as they were largely dependent on the US economy, the European economies. The worst depression in human history had begun. It lasted for years and there didn't seem to be an end to it.

The economist John Maynard Keynes explained why: Due to the crisis, many people had lost their job. The unemployment rate was at a record high. This meant that many people didn't have any money to buy things and those that still had money didn't spend it with full hands as there was always the risk that they would be next without a job.

As the demand was low, the industry didn't invest in new products and kept the production low. This made even more people jobless with the results that the demand kept on declining. The economy was trapped in a vicious circle of declining demand and declining supply.

Keynes made the proposal that this vicious circle could only be broken if the state stepped in and created demand. He should start building streets, houses and other infrastructure and thus create a demand for workers. These workers would then have the money which would allow them to increase the demand for consumer goods. The industry would then use this money to increase its production, hire more people, and thus the vicious circle could be broken.

Left to itself, the economy would stay in the recession. And it was thanks to Keynes program that the United States, Germany and other countries where the state actively took measures to create demand finally left the recession.

As a result of the success of Keynes intervention economics, the politicians had learnt that they needed to interfere in the economy to assure that the workers would get a fair share of the wealth generated by the economy. This fair distribution against the will of the majority of the upper class was after all the guarantee for the economic boom of the second industrial revolution.

To assure a fair distribution of the newly generated wealth of the second industrial revolution, the state created social security nets and assured workers' rights in a way it had never done before. But as the wealth for all increased, not even the upper class complained. And the organization which is now disrespectfully called "welfare state" was born.

Welfare state meant that nobody had to fear poverty anymore when he lost a job or got ill. Social security would take care of him and help him until he was back on track. Everything was fine until the economy saturated.

Nobody blamed the economic recession of the 1970s on the saturated market. Some say it was due to the oil crisis (which happened later, as we have already discussed) and some say there is another villain who is to blame: The state.

The state had interfered into the economy. Not as much as in a communist country where the state controlled the economy. But the state of the western nations had reduced the freedom of the companies and the upper class when it increased the freedom of the workers. For this is what happens when two groups are playing on the same field:

one group has to make room if the other group shall get more. If the state makes sure that certain rights for the workers are protected, then he reduces the freedom of the rich to treat the workers as they like.

And it was this interference, according to some economists, that was the root cause for the recession of the 1970s. Left to itself, as Adam Smith had proposed, the economy would never have entered into a recession or would have left it much faster.

The economists who supported that view were called neo-liberals, as they referred to Adam Smith's liberal views in their works. Their statement was clear: The state should not interfere with the economy. How the consumer economy would have taken off without the state interfering and improving the lot of the workers (for only some entrepreneurs like Henry Ford understood that they needed the worker) is something that these economists cannot explain. And neither can they explain how a saturated economy should be able to show growth-rates as it had shown right after the Second World War. But neo-liberalism is less a scientific subject then more a kind of belief. And the important thing is that the politicians believed that these economists were right.

To be fair, the politicians didn't really have a choice. The ideas of the neo-liberals (like the idea that the state should no longer interfere with the economy) were suddenly heard from all sides. Hundreds of economists repeated this mantra and public magazines wrote about it. Everyone seemed to believe it, even though there were no proofs. But that is how belief works.

And even the economists didn't have a real choice but to support the neo-liberal idea that would play into the hands of the upper class as it would remove their greatest opponent: The state. After all, the economists need to do research, but if you want to do research nowadays at a university, you need to raise funds from private donors. And there are not many private donors who can give you thousands of dollars for research. There might be some unions and left-winged parties that can spend the money, but the main donors are companies, steered by members of the upper class. And guess what they would like to hear…

If economists wanted to succeed in their carrier, they had to do research. To do research, they needed the support of companies. So in the end, economists said what the upper class wanted to hear, and the magazines published what the upper class (who incidentally owned them) wanted to read. And the politicians did what seemed to be right because everybody said so (apart from some crackpots you couldn't take seriously).

That's how neo-liberalism became the mainstream in all major industrialized countries. It started with the UK and USA in the 1980s, and finally reached Germany. Here it had to wait until Gerhard Schröder had become chancellor because Helmut Kohl had a rather pragmatic view on this topic. When asked why he didn't support a more neo-liberal, company-friendly politics, he simply asked back: How many votes do they have?

But these times went by, and neo-liberalism took over. The mantra of this economical theory is simple: Less state. This is the only way the upper class can regain control over the society. After all, it was the workers' friendly state that enacted so many laws that restricted the freedom of the upper class. With a powerless state, this problem would vanish by itself.

The politics of neo-liberalism were similar in all countries. It was a two way strategy: First, you support the performers; second, you punish the fainéants.

The tricky question was: How should we separate the performers from the fainéants? But the answer comes easy to any economist. An economist thinks that you get all information about a product from its price. If the price is high, then you have a good product, if the price is low, then you can assume that the product has a low quality. If you transfer this thinking to the labor world, you can assume that those, who earn a lot of money, are the performers, and those, who don't earn much money or nothing at all, are the fainéants. Life can be simple.

Now you want to support the performers. As these are the people who earn a lot of money, you simply reduce the taxes for the rich. The United States under Ronald Reagan reduced the top tax rates for the rich from more than 70% to below 40%. Germany under Gerhard Schröder reduced the top tax rates from 53% to 42%. And those, who don't work at all but only make their money by cashing in dividends and interests, are obviously extremely high performers, so the state reduced their top tax rate to 25%. We could need more of these people.

At the same time, the state attacked the lazy people. First of all, he made clear that they are lazy; their only goal in life seems to be to live on social security for the rest of their life. This is, of course, unfair, so they need to be punished. The social security was reduced significantly and can be reduced to virtually nothing if they still refuse to work. And the work they have to do isn't necessarily what they once learned or a job that pays roughly what they used to earn in earlier jobs. A job that those lazy fainéants have to take is any job that is offered to them, even if it means that an engineer has to clean toilets.

With such a pressure on the unemployed (but be fair: They deserved it), the companies did all they could to help. They created thousands of new jobs. Okay, the jobs were only temporary appointments and paid only a fraction of comparable jobs. But the unemployed had to take them and were removed from the unemployment statistics. This was considered to be a big success – apart from those who were now working in the "low-wage sector" with no perspective of leaving it again (for who would hire an engineer who has cleaned toilets for some years?).

But politics, supported by neo-liberal economists, stated that we would need this low-wage sector to be competitive in a globalized world. Roughly one quarter of all people in the United States, UK and Germany are now working in this low-wage sector. You have to pay the price if you want to be competitive and survive.

But you might wonder if the low-wage sector is really needed for competitive reasons. If you take a look at jobs where more than two third of all employees in Germany are getting low wages, then you find taxi-drivers, building cleaners, hairdressers, waiters, sales assistants and so on. None of them is working in a job where you have international competition (at least I never thought of flying to China to get my hair cut). There is only one reason why we have a low wage sector: Increase profits for the upper class.

The consequences of this politics that supports the performers (i.e. the upper class) and punishes the fainéants (i.e. all the rest) are easy to see: The gap between the rich and the poor is getting wider and wider in the industrialized countries.

The growing inequality and poverty of large parts of the population can be measured with the Gini coefficient. The coefficient was invented by the Italian statistician Corrado Gini, and it provides a simple way to describe how the income or the wealth is distributed within a country.

In a perfect communist society, the Gini coefficient would be 0. Everyone just owns and earns the same. Even the communist countries never reached that goal – and such a distribution of wealth would probably be considered unfair by most of us. Why should someone, who is only working one hour per day earn as much as someone who is working ten hours a day?

The other extreme would be a Gini coefficient of 1. This would be a society where nobody owns or earns anything – apart from one man who owns and earns all the money. That would be a perfect tyranny, and surely not a society you would want to live in.

A Gini coefficient that would fit to a fair society should be somewhere in between. In fact, for most of the time after the Second World War, the Gini coefficient for income distribution in America was around 0.3. The same number we can find for most European countries like France, England or Germany.

The higher the Gini coefficient the more unequal is the distribution of the income. The Brazilian economy was dominated by a handful of great land owners with the majority of the people living in great poverty for most of their time. The people didn't have access to a good education, they didn't have access to good jobs, and they didn't have the possibility to improve their life. This has only changed recently. But up to this point the Gini coefficient for Brazil was one of the highest in the world: 0.6.

History thus shows us that we don't have to reach a Gini coefficient of 1 to live in an unjust country. The rather low number of 0.6 is sufficient. A rather just distribution of income and wealth seems to be reached when the Gini coefficient is in the range of 0.3. The jackpot question now is: What is the Gini coefficient for income of the USA at the beginning of the 21st century? It is an astonishing 0.47. Germany's Gini coefficient has risen from 0.25 to above 0.3, and practically all other industrialized countries show the same development. Our countries become more and more unfair and unequal. The development of the 20th century with a growing middle class that overcame the poverty of the lower class has been stopped – and reversed. The middle class is dying. The upper class is trying to feather its own nest and doesn't care a bit about the rest of the society. The incomes of the middle class are stagnating or even shrinking, while the incomes of the upper class are reaching new record heights. This can be seen for instance on the Forbes list of the 400 richest people in the world. You needed "only" 92 million dollars in 1982 to make it on that list. In the year 2000, your minimum wealth had to be 725 million dollars to enter the list.

At the same time, more and more people from the middle class are first losing their jobs, and then their homes. Today, it became quite easy to move from the middle of the society to its lower end, while the superrich are taking baths in Champagne.

And although the tax rates for the rich have been reduced to a ridiculous minimum, they are still trying to avoid paying taxes and are moving their wealth to tax havens like Switzerland or the Bermudas. No industrialized country would have to make debts if the rich would pay their taxes. As they are not available, the state is trying to get its money from the middle class as its members do not have the possibility to move their wealth to tax havens. Banks will only help you with this task if you want to transfer some millions; they don't offer their job to those who only have a few thousand.

But this can't go on, can it?

The last brazenness was the financial crisis. Greedy bankers, who had made millions during their time, had brought several banks and the worldwide economy close to a breakdown. Billions and billions of dollars had to be spent by the state (a.k.a. the tax-payer a.k.a. the middle class) to bail-out the bankrupt banks. The bankers didn't see the necessity to join them, nor did the investors of the upper class who had earned billions while the game was still running.

And now, that the worst seems to be over? Do we see that the bankers and investors try to behave and act responsible?

Not in the least. They continue as if nothing had happened. And, in fact, nothing had happened, at least not to them. They hadn't lost anything, and they can be sure: If it will happen again, they will have their money safe, and the state will pay. They got the permission to behave immorally. And you can be sure that they will use it.

But this should have consequence, shouldn't it? The middle class, after all, is not just a nobody. The middle class is the strongest force in a democracy. It just has to raise its voice and let those lousy bastards know that it is enough! It just has to raise its voice and tell the upper class that it won't tolerate their anti-social behavior any longer! It just has to raise its voice and let everyone know who the leader of the pack is!

But, shh, be quite. Do you hear something?

There is nothing. Some mumbling, maybe, but nobody stands up to stop it. And the mumbling may be caused by those who have already lost, by those who already slipped down to the lower class. But maybe it isn't. In general, they have given up. Their grandfathers hoped that things could get better, so they fought for it. Today we know that things can only get worse. And those who experienced it have lost all interest in our society. They form a part of the society that no longer belongs to it.

And the rest of the middle class doesn't seem to be really interested of what's going on. Don't they understand? They should understand it, because they feel the consequences of neo-liberal politics every day. Maybe they just close their eyes and hope destiny will pass by if they don't look.

That is the only hope left. For if everything has been running smoothly for some time, do you want to know if a storm is coming? So maybe they understand, but they don't want to understand.

And sometimes you get the impression that the middle class doesn't really feel affect by the problem. After all, the problems touch the poor, not the rich. And who in the middle class would admit that he is poor? They are no longer part of the lower class, they made it, they are rich, and they are part of the upper class.

Poor idiots. The upper class is a closed society. They distribute the well-paid and important jobs in our countries among themselves; no-one from the outside can easily enter this exclusive club, and definitely not millions of people who define themselves as the middle class.

The middle class is an upgraded lower class, nothing more. Everything that is bad for the lower class is also bad for the middle class. Only the middle class thinks it is part of the upper class – and thus applauds any politics that improves the situation for the rich (reduction of the top income tax rate), and doesn't really care about politics that worsens the situation for the poor.

This self-delusion is the greatest enemy of the middle class, because it prevents them to clearly see what's going on. And thus they are happily digging their own grave, with the upper class drinking champagne and dancing on it.

Trust in Technology – but not blindly

Technology Improves Our Lives

Let us start this little essay with something that Albert Einstein called a "thought experiment", because it could not – or only with difficulties – be realized in real life. Let us imagine two men who have access to some sort of time machine that could only bring them from their present to a pre-defined future.

The first man lived in the Roman Empire at the time of the emperor Augustus (around the time of Christ's birth). The time machine brings him to the year 1517, the same year that Martin Luther nailed his 95 theses on the door of the All Saints' Church in Wittenberg. The second man already lived in this year and is transported into the year 2013 by the time machine.

The first man made a jump of fifteen centuries the second man only covered five centuries. But who of them would feel more at home in his new time – and who of them would think he landed on a strange planet?

Although the big time difference might lead us on a wrong track, it is probably save to say that the first man who moved from Roman times to the Renaissance would be more at home than the man who only jumped five centuries. The clothes of the Renaissance might have been completely different from what he knew from his time. The Romans wore tunics while trousers were the clothes of the Barbarian tribes up in the North of Europe. So he might be shocked to see his countrymen wearing the clothes of the Barbarians. In addition, the shirts of the rich were more fanciful than everything the Romans had known at their time.

The clothes of the Renaissance resembled in their playful appearance the huge and seemingly weightless cathedrals of the Gothic art. The Romans were also skilful builders, many of their buildings survived until today, but their buildings were heavy and looked much more massive than the fragile looking cathedrals of the Renaissance – although they topped everything in height the Romans had built.

But apart from these artistic differences, the time traveler might have felt quite at home. The people of the Renaissance were still traveling on horseback and in coaches as they did during the times of the Roman Empire. And the majority of the people traveled on foot as they could afford neither horse nor coach. The weapons of the soldiers would also have been familiar to the Roman visitor: They were fighting mainly with swords and spears, just like their ancestors back in Rome. The first guns and canons had been invented by that time, but were only rarely seen and had not yet replaced the weaponry of ancient times.

The landscape was mainly rural; most of the people were working on the fields. Here and there, some cities existed, but they had only just grown back to the strength they had already possessed during Roman times. During the Dark Ages and the Middles Ages the cities had seen a steady decline and decay, and this development was only recently reversed (although our time traveler wouldn't know this detail). Most of the people lived in small villages. The temples of Roman times were replaced by churches, and the people no longer believed in a Heaven full of Gods, but only one almighty and all-knowing God. Although this concept might have been strange to the visitor from Roman times, he was well aware that people in other regions had different believes. After all, the Romans had conquered strange countries in large numbers to become aware of that fact. And they didn't mind, as long as the newly conquered countries paid taxes to Rome. And even Jesus Christ didn't object to that.

The science of the Renaissance was the science of the Greek, recently re-discovered by curious philosophers in central Europe. It wanted to explain the world with logic, but was still trapped in a world of superstition and esotericism, halfway between pure religion and pure science. But that wouldn't have been new for a Roman. After all, this military civilization had taken most of its education from the Greek, and only translated into Latin.

Even talking to the people of the Renaissance wouldn't have been a problem for our time traveler. Latin was still the language of the upper class. All scientific books and even novels and poems were written in Latin. It wasn't understood by the lower classes, so the upper class could keep all their knowledge hidden from the people. But even in Roman times only the upper class of the conquered countries spoke Latin. The lower class only had to perform its work.

So apart from some minor differences, our time traveler from Roman times would have felt quite at home in the times of the Renaissance.

This is completely different for the man from the Renaissance who travels to our times. This man would feel like being stranded on a strange planet. He would find houses that were taller than the church spires. He would find himself on the side of streets that are occupied by huge metallic, coach-like objects that were moving all by themselves, without any horses and much faster than anything he knew. On a first glance you could have the impression that these objects had taken control and were now the dominating species on earth.

He would meet people on the street looking at little boxes that play music without any musicians nearby. And sometimes the people talk to these boxes – and the boxes answer! In some areas, he would be able to see huge, silvery birds flying over his head like creatures from fairy tales. He wouldn't understand that these objects are just results of human technology, that they have been created by man. He would assume that somehow magic has entered the world and the limits between the Heavens and Earth have somehow vanished, for any sufficiently advanced technology is indistinguishable from magic, as the science fiction writer Arthur C. Clarke once wrote.

But these changes are not due to magic; they are not miracles. They are men-made, although someone from the Renaissance wouldn't understand it. In fact, the changes in human understanding and technology we could experience in just a few centuries are breath-taking.

It all started, when men like Galileo Galilei or Nicolaus Copernicus started to ask some questions about the world we live in. Is it really the center of the world? Is the sun really moving around the earth? The Bible was clear about it: The sun was moving around the earth. In the Book of Joshua we can even read that Joshua made the sun stand still (so it had to be moving the rest of the time). Questioning the structure of our universe was also questioning the reliability of the Bible, it was questioning religion.

The church didn't like it and forced Galileo to openly admit that the earth doesn't move around the sun (on his death-bed, however, he presumably said: And it does move). But the seeds were sown. And men like Newton and Laplace nourished them. Newton founded physics with his fundamental laws of mechanics, and Laplace once wrote a book about the universe in which he not even once mentioned God. Once God and the religion had been the central force in human life; now they were not even mentioned in a book about the universe. When asked by Napoleon, why he had written a book about the universe without mentioning God even once, Laplace simply answered: "I didn't need this hypothesis."

Science had destroyed the dogma and superstition of religion. It had paved the way to a modern society. This way was started by some giants, but it was continued by thousands of scientists and engineers who based on the scientific rules and used them to build steam engines, cars, planes, transistors, computers and thousands of other things that would look like a kind of magic to someone from the 16th century.

Science and technology have made our lives so much easier. In ancient times, all people had to work hard to gain a miserable income and be barely able to survive, i.e. those that were working; those that weren't working and only owned the land the farmers were working on had a much more easier live. Now the work is mainly done by machines, although there are still some people who have to work hard with their hands. But for most of the workers, the hard physical work is only remembered in stories from the old days.

Even though the aristocracy was much better off when it came to working conditions (they simply had none), the situation was almost identical for workers and the aristocracy when it came to health conditions. The mortality rate among workers might have been somewhat higher than among the aristocracy (especially among the children, as it was the high mortality rate of children that caused the low average age of these times; once you had made it to adulthood your chance to survive to an old age was almost as high as today), but the difference wasn't big –

especially when compared to the very low mortality rate that we have today.

The reasons for this were the lamentably sanitary conditions. We take it for granted that we only have to open the water-tap and have access to clean water and that there is at least one toilet in each apartment. But this is a very recent development. In former times, people were taking their water from public wells which regularly only provided water of a very dubious quality. And even the very rich didn't have toilets in their homes. King Louis XIV might have built the most fabulous castle of modern times, the Castle of Versailles, but even this extravagant and magnificent building didn't have a bathroom. If you were in need of a quite space for your basic needs, you simply used a dark corner or empty staircase. Versailles in spite of its entire splendor was stinking like a garbage dump. That's why perfumes of all kinds were very popular in these times, even among men.

It was thanks to improved sanitary conditions and better healthcare that the mortality rate decreased drastically. This caused other problems – the army of unemployed poor during the industrial revolution, the army of starving people – but in the course of time, technology could also solve these problems with improved agricultural technologies and fertilizers that increased the yields drastically. Today food is available in such amounts to humans who always lived in scarcity throughout their history that we have to deal with another problem: Obesity. Our bodies store all the food we can eat in anticipation of bad times – but thanks to technology there are no bad times anymore. You could complain about it, but nobody would think you were serious. A famine to reduce your weight would really be too drastic a diet.

Science and technology were able to make these advancements because they wanted to know. Religion is happy when it can believe. It will never question the Revelation and the Holy Books. Science will. That's why religions at all times had their problems with science and scientist. Scientists cannot simply believe if it is absurd or in contradiction to experience. Scientists are critical minds. They want to understand why they should believe something; they want to know if it can be really correct. Spoken with a religious background in mind, you could say that scientist think that God gave us brains to think – and not only to learn religious texts by heart.

Only when you ask questions you will find out that against all appearance and against everything it says in the Bible, it is in fact the earth that is moving around the sun and not the other way round. Only when you dare to ask questions, you will improve the human situation. And you will never ask questions if you already believe to be in the possession of everything there is to know. But if you wonder why the apple is falling to the ground, you have done the first step into eternal, religious damnation – but eternal, human salvation.

The scientific approach is a deeply human approach. It is not only human because humans are curious beings, they want to know, they ask questions (remember all the questions little children have once they learn to speak?). But science teaches you humbleness, it teaches you tolerance, because science tells you that you don't know everything – and that you can be wrong. Only if you understand that your way can be wrong, you start looking for the right way. Continuing on the wrong way despite all evidence is something that can be done by every idiot. But it needs a very smart mind to understand what is the wrong way and what is the right way. It needs a very smart mind like the mind of Socrates, one of the greatest philosophers of all times, to come to this insight: "I know that I know nothing."

The religious dogma, on the other hand, is. "I know everything. And you better agree, because contradiction can be hazardous to your life."

If religion had kept its dominance throughout the Dark Ages up to our times, if Martin Luther hadn't questioned the religious dogmas, if scientists hadn't developed their method of theory and experiment to understand the world, then we would still be living in the Dark Ages. And this was the time when the Roman civilization got lost in Europe, when the Europeans forgot everything the Greek had discovered, when the Europeans unlearned the ability to build huge buildings like the Romans did, when, in short, the human civilization fell back by several centuries.

If this had been our future, then the time traveler from the 16th century wouldn't have felt like being on a strange planet when visiting the 21st century, a planet where magic seems to be available to everyone. Rather he would have felt like having gone back in time, to a time before humans had invented civilization.

We should be lucky that science and technology have changed our world so much.

Two Sides of the Medal

Art is always a mirror of its time. The artists of the Middle Ages were trapped in a superstitious thinking and didn't see the world as it was; science hadn't been rediscovered yet. So they didn't paint the world as it could be seen, but they painted the world as it appeared to them. The things that were important became a prominent place in their pictures and were big. Things that were less important were only painted at the side and very small, even though they might have been much bigger in real life than the things that were important to the painters.

All this changed in the Renaissance. The perspective was introduced in the paintings, and the world was shown as it really was, with an almost scientific interest in details, as can be seen in the masterpieces of Flemish artists.

After the industrial revolution, when technology had shaped the look of the world, artists became interested in the capabilities of technology. What would the human race be able to achieve with technology in the next years? What seemingly miraculous features would appear?

The artists that started to ask these questions were writers. One of the first who wrote such "science fiction" books was the French writer Jules Verne who lived in the 19th century. His books like "Twenty Thousands Leagues under the Sea" and "From Earth to Moon" are classics because they give an astonishingly accurate description of machines that would only be constructed decades or a whole century later.

In his book "Twenty Thousands Leagues under the Sea", Jules Verne tells the story of captain Nemo and his huge submarine, the Nautilus. It was impossible to construct such a huge submarine at the time of Jules Verne, but there were first examples of bringing men under the sea-level in small submarines. And maybe someday they would be bigger, just like trains were getting faster and faster almost every year. There seemed to be no limit to technology, everything seemed possible, and Jules Verne was sharing this optimism when designing the Nautilus in his thoughts.

In his book "From Earth to Moon", Jules Verne was even more daring – but nevertheless astonishingly precise. It was years before the Brother Wright did their first flight with an airplane in 1903, but Jules Verne obviously didn't think there would be a limit to human technology. It was already conquering the land and the sea, so it would only be a question of time when it would conquer the air – and finally the heavens. It should be possible that man is travelling through the air, so it should also be possible that he is travelling to the moon.

And again, Jules Verne got some details right, like the fact that rockets start close to the equator to profit from the high rotational speed. Only no-one ever constructed a huge gun to fire the astronauts into the sky, they simply used a controlled explosion in a rocket. But even though Jules Verne made some mistakes, his prophecies about the future were better than the prophecies written down by Nostradamus.

But that was because he relied on technology and simply took an optimistic view about what technology could achieve.

This optimistic view, however, wasn't shared for long. It changed in only one generation.

The protagonist of this change was H.G. Wells, who was born in the second half of the 19th century. Maybe he was already influenced by the worker's movement that had made it clear to everyone that the brand new world of the industrial revolution did not only bring advantages to the human race – at least not to the workers who suffered more than any human generation before.

H.G. Wells depicted a more negative picture of a technology based future in his books. He was not only optimistic like Jules Verne who never stopped marveling at what humans could do thanks to modern technology and science. When Jules Verne was thinking about traveling through space and conquering new planets like the moon,

H.G. Wells took this idea one step further: Maybe not only humans were traveling through space to other planets, but aliens from other planets might be traveling to earth as well. And you only had to look at human history to see that travelers arriving in alien countries were not always friendly to the indigenous population, as the native Americans, the "Indians", could tell – well, at least those that had survived the visits of the European conquistadores.

Playing on this idea, H.G. Wells wrote the novel "The War of the Worlds" which describes the invasion of earth by Martians. In spite of all our technology and science, the war against the aliens is lost even before it really started. In some sort of early blitzkrieg the Martians take over the earth and defeat the human armies. This seems to be the end of the human race, but the war against the Martians is finally won. The Martians, however, were not defeated by the superior human technology. They lost their fight against the seemingly most insignificant life forms on earth: Bacteria. The immune system of the Martians wasn't able to fight them, so they simply died, just like the Indians died of diseases the Europeans had imported to America.

H.G. Wells describes another pessimistic view of our future in his novel "The Time Machine". The book describes the travels of a man into a far distant future, several thousand years from now. In this future, he meets the peaceful Eloi. They live in peace with nature and seem to have everything they need in abundance. Man seems to have reached finally what he lost shortly after creation: Paradise on earth.

But the time traveler soon finds out that this Paradise has a very dark side. This dark side lives underground and feeds on the Elois. The Morlocks are another human race that masters technology and hides in caves far away from the sun and nature. The Morlocks are heartless and inhuman creatures that only slightly remind the time traveler of their human ancestors. They look more like bidedal animals.

Living with nature preserved humanity, living with technology and away from nature destroyed it. Technology is not only good.

In fact, one can safely say that neither the optimistic view of Jules Verne nor the pessimistic view expressed by H.G. Wells provides a complete and fair description of technology. Science and technology has two sides, just like a medal. They have improved our lives significantly and nobody could say that he would be willing to live without it from one minute to another. The human race was much too eager to change its life to a modern, technology based lifestyle. And this did not only happen in the past, even today indigenous groups that used to life like their ancestors in the stone-age are only too happy to embrace the new lifestyle. It is simply too tempting and it offers too many advantages.

But there are drawbacks to science and technology that we tend to ignore, which is extremely problematic in our times when the technology we use is so powerful that it can erase whole cities within seconds. Nevertheless we use these technologies with a surprising naivety, like children playing with dangerous goods and not caring about the consequences.

And sometimes small reasons can have huge consequences. The killing of the Archduke Franz Ferdinand of Austria in 1914 led to the First World War and the killing of millions of people. Some seemingly harmless chemicals like the chlorofluorocarbons led to the destruction of the ozone layer above the poles and an increased risk for skin cancer in southern and northern countries.

Modern societies and nature are extremely complex structures, where features interact and reinforce in ways that no-one can predict. This is the realm of chaos theory which is known for the statement that the wing beat of a butterfly in Brazil might lead to thunderstorms in Europe.

Everything around us is heavily linked with each other. A small change might lead to a small tipping of the scales – or it might turn them over. In general, you will not be able to make a correct prediction. Nature is much too complex to be understood with the simple law of cause and effect.

The thing even becomes more complicated as the effect is sometimes so far away that we don't see it or the effect is visible but the connection to the cause is well hidden. In both cases, we are unable to connect cause and effect and wonder what's happening – or don't even bother as we don't see the effect.

In spite of these limitations of our knowledge and understanding, we are still using new technologies as if nothing could happen, only because we think that nothing has happen, for we haven't seen the effect.

But there are severe side effects.

The Side Effects of Technology

When you are asked about the greatest achievements of modern technology, you might think of tall skyscrapers that literally scratch at the sky, or planes that flight with several times the speed of sound or ships that are so big that they could house a small city; you might think of computers that allow us to communicate with the other side of the world within fractions of a second, or download whole movies in minutes. But would you think that soap is one of the biggest inventions of mankind?

We already mentioned this early: One of the biggest steps forward in human civilization has been the victory in the battle against bacteria and other pathogenic germs. They are everywhere. There is a philosophical question about the number of angels that can dance on the tip of the needle. I can't answer that, but the tip of the needle is big enough to provide living area for thousands of bacteria. And they have killed far more men than man has killed his own kind. Only with improved sanitary conditions did the average life-expectancy improve. Without detergents, our children would still die in high numbers. And not only would the children die.

Only some decades ago, young mothers died in large numbers shortly after they had given birth to a child. This wasn't caused by the strain of the birth, but it somehow seemed connected. The Hungarian doctor Ignaz Semmelweis found the answer in the 19th century: The mothers died because they were touched by their doctors during the check-up. These doctors had touched all kinds of sick men during the day and sometimes they even had performed an autopsy before they had a look at the mothers. But they didn't wash their hands before they visited the mothers. So they transferred the bacteria they had collected during the day to the women who were weakened by the strains of birth – they fell sick and eventually died. Ignaz Semmelweis could show that the simple procedure of washing your hands before having a look at the mothers could reduce the occurrence of puerperal fever to almost naught. This should have been a huge breakthrough.

However, the doctors quickly understood the implications of Semmelweis' theory: If he were right, then this would mean that the doctors who were supposed to cure the patients from their diseases were in fact causing it. And this simply couldn't be true. In addition: Simply washing your hands to save people from dying seemed such a ridiculously simply solution that it couldn't be true. It couldn't be what shouldn't be, so the doctors ignored Semmelweis' warnings for years, and many more women had to die until the medical community finally accepted the fact that washing your hands and thus killing thousands of little germs could save lives.

Today, nobody questions the importance of a good hygiene. And the use of detergents and soap has probably saved more lives than the application of penicillin, although the life-saving qualities of penicillin are more obvious as you can see how a sick person becomes healthy; in the case of detergents, healthy persons stay healthy – so there is no direct proof of its effectiveness.

And the effectiveness of detergents strongly depends on the water that is being used. Some minerals like calcium, magnesium and other metal cations, that make the water hard, reduce their effectiveness. But to every problem there is a solution. If metallic cations reduce the effectiveness of detergents, then simply remove them from the water. As filtering the water would be too expensive and complicated, chemists found another solution: They added phosphates to the detergents. They bind the metal cations and thus remove them as an active substance from the water.

With phosphates added to the detergents, the effectiveness of detergents remained unaffected and as a side-effect the damage caused to plumbing due to lime scale was also significantly reduced. Adding phosphates to detergents made the production of the detergents slightly more complex, but in the end there only seemed to be advantages when using them. So they were largely used for decades; millions of tons of phosphates were added to the detergents.

The problem was that in the process of washing the phosphates would be taken away through the drains and into the rivers. Sewage plants were not able to remove them effectively – and in the beginning no-one even tried. So the phosphates made it to our rivers and lakes, and caused a surprising effect. Surprising in the sense that it was surprising nobody had thought that it could happen.

It was known that phosphates are very effective fertilizers. They had been used in agriculture long before they were used as additives in detergents. Practically every farmer used them on his fields. So it was surprising that nobody had thought that they might not only be effective fertilizers on fields but also in the water.

The water is not always clear, even if it might seem to. Millions of little animals, plants and algae are living in there, too small for the eye to see. When phosphates supported the growth of plants on land they even more effectively supported the growth of plants and algae in the water, as they virtually surrounded them. The algae population almost exploded and consumed all the nutritive substances in the waters. No other life-form could compete with the doped algae. While the algae prospered, the others simply died. By improving the detergents, man was fertilizing huge parts of the waters in the rivers and lakes – where life simply died.

This seems to be the running joke of human technology: We find a simple technical solution for a technical problem – and cause even more problems with it.

This is even more astounding as we knew that phosphates are effective fertilizers. We could have imagined the problem just by taking some time and think about it. But then: Would we ever have imagined that we could kill life and depopulate whole rivers and lakes by fertilizing them?

And in many cases the consequences of our actions are even less obvious then they are in the case of the phosphates. Sometimes it takes years after we have started to use a new technology before the side-effects of it become visible.

One example are the chlorofluorocarbons (CFCs). Thomas Midgley, who was working for General Motors at the beginning of the 20th century, synthesized them in his lab while he was looking for some safe refrigerant. The CFCs seemed to be the perfect solution: They are chemically inert, i.e. they practically do not react with other substances; they are practically inflammable (which most of the refrigerants used at that time were not) and not toxic. Thomas Midgley himself proved the harmlessness of the CFCs in a spectacular experiment: He inhaled them public and survived the experiment completely unharmed.

The experiment was even more spectacular if you know something more about Thomas Midgley: Some years before the invention of the CFCs, Midgley had invented a substance called tetraethyllead which was added to gasoline as an inexpensive octane booster. This substance, however, contained lead. And everybody knew that lead is not safe for human consumption. In can cause diseases of the nervous system. In fact, many workers at a production site of tetraethyllaed suffered from hallucinations in which they believed to see little insects everywhere. The production site was name "the house of butterflies" and tetraethyllead got the nickname "loony gas" by the press.

To restore the good name of his invention, Thomas Midgley called a press conference and publicly inhaled tetraethyllead. As he suffered no immediate side-effects, the press announced that the substance was safe for human consumption, and the industry could use it for many decades, polluting our environment with the toxic lead.

It was only known many years later that Thomas Midgley had to recover from severe lead-poisoning in the following year. This makes it even more remarkable that some years later Thomas Midgley performed the same stunt with the CFCs. By the way: With tetraethyllead and CFCs on his account, there is probably no other human being that influenced the earth's atmosphere as deeply as Thomas Midgley.

But coming back to Midgley public experiment: The CFCs were really safe for human consumption. He didn't have to recover from a severe case of poisoning this time. Thus, the CFCs were largely used as refrigerants, blowing agents or degreasing solvents. Billions of tons of CFC have been produced and released into our environment. Why should a special care be taken, as they were completely harmless? So our atmosphere served as a dustbin for CFCs, just like our streets are dustbins for smokers.

Just to repeat it: This was not considered to be a problem as the CFCs were chemically inert. They could live for more than a hundred years before they decayed. But as out atmosphere is so huge, even with all the tons of CFCs released into the atmosphere, the relative amount of the CFCs is still negligible.

It was only in the 1970s when it became clear that the most attractive feature of the CFCs, their low reactivity, was the key to their most destructive effect. As CFCs were able to survive unchanged for more than a hundred years in the earth's atmosphere, they were able to travel to its upper levels; they were able to travel to the upper stratosphere. Up there, the sun's ultraviolet radiation, however, is strong enough to crack the chemical bonds of the CFCs and release the chlorine. And chlorine is anything but a harmless element, that's why it is used in our drinking water and in public baths to kill germs. Chlorine is very reactive.

In the upper atmosphere, it instantly reacts with the ozone, reducing it to simple oxygen – and then moves on to the next ozone molecule to repeat the feat. One chlorine atom can destroy thousands of ozone molecules.

Ozone is considered to be a nuisance on ground level, where it teases the respiratory system, but in the stratosphere ozone is protecting us against the harmful ultraviolet rays of the sun. Without this protection, mankind would have probably died of skin cancer by now.

The theory of the 1970s, that CFCs could damage the ozone layer, was proved to be correct in the 1980s when dramatic reductions in the thickness of the ozone layers above the poles were observed. For several months per year, the ozone concentration is reduced by more than 50 percent, and the size of this "hole" was increasing, reaching the southern parts of Australia and the northern parts of Europe.

In a very fast move, the nations of the world decided to ban CFCs in the 1990s. Since then, the ozone holes above the poles have recovered, but they can still be observed. It might take decades or even centuries before the ozone layer recovers completely, after all the CFCs were chosen for their chemical stability.

And they were not the only man-made substance hailed for its indestructibility. Another example is plastics. They do not decay like plants within a few days, even exposed to water for a long time, they do not show any deterioration. Again, they seem to be perfect materials, easy to form, everlasting and cheap. Just like CFCs they can easily last a century – and just like CFCs they can be found everywhere by now.

We might not see them everywhere, but this is not because a certain square meter of land might be free of plastic, it's only because plastic has been reduced to small grains – too small for the eye to see. Traces of plastic can be found in every square meter of sand on the beach, they can be found in our cities, in the tundra of Siberia, the rain forests of the Amazon and even at the poles. We can even find traces of plastic in the air that we breathe. They are everywhere.

You might think that I am exaggerating when I saying that we can find plastic in the air that we breathe. I would be happy if you were right. But the official numbers tell us that the usually intake through the air of the artificial substance Vinyl chloride is more than one tenth of a microgram, each day. And it is not the only artificial substance in the air that we breathe.

But plastic is mainly gathering in our waters. Why not, after all there's a lot of it on earth. The countless rivers are taking the small plastic particles to the seas. Some ships are even right on the spot to dump them directly into the sea. Ocean currents are taking the particles with them and collecting them in huge maelstroms of trash. One of the biggest can be found between Hawaii and the American mainland. It has the size of Central Europe.

The maelstroms of plastic in the oceans around the world are nourished by the plastics we use in all the products of our daily life (try to imagine what your daily life would look like if you didn't use plastic). And they keep on growing as plastic lasts for a long time before it finally decays into small and harmless molecules.

The maelstroms are not only nourished by daily products like plastic bags or bottles, but also by tiny plastic grains that are contained in many sanitary product like shampooing or shower gels. Their purpose is to rub the dirt from our skin. These small particles can't be filtered out in the sewage plants, so they go directly to the sea. On their way, they collect toxic substances on their surface before they are eaten by plankton and other small creatures of the sea. The small creatures are eaten by bigger ones and by fish and finally by huge animals like seals. So you can find plastic in the stomachs of every animal, from the smallest to the biggest. While accumulating plastic particles, the animals also accumulated the harmful substances that had been collected on the surface of the tiny grains of plastic. Many fish caught in the sea show toxic contamination well above the threshold values. And these values are generally not measured before the fish end up on our plates...

But mankind strives on, oblivious of past mistakes. Now it tries not only to form matter, now it tries to form life itself.

To be precise: It is not new that man tries to modify life on earth. He has done this since the beginning of civilization. After all, he always believed, in all modesty, to be the image of God. And that's only a small step away from actually believing to be God.

What has changed over time is the technology used to change nature. In the beginning, man didn't use a sophisticated approach, he simply copied nature: He selected those animals and plants that suited him best and made sure they reproduced in great numbers. Breeding was man's answer to natural selection. And this approach was quite successful. We can't remember it, but the full corn or high yielding wheat that we find on our fields today could not be found in nature. The natural ancestors had tiny grains in such a low number that it would never have been enough to feed man. But we took our times, and in the course of centuries we had changed the plants into a direction where they yielded the biggest profit.

And man also changed animals. The most significant change he achieved is with the wolf. He turned it from a wild beast into a submissive companion that ranges from the huge Saint Bernard to the little dachshund. Just by using the simply technology of breeding, you can create a huge variety of life forms.

But there is one drawback to breeding: It takes a long time. Differences in size and features have to be detected and combined, and only in the next generation you will see if the combination was successful. It takes generations to improve the plants and animals into products that we can use profitably. And sometimes we will never reach our goals as nature has a tendency to be unpredictable. So man looked for a technology that would improve his control over the outcome and speed up the process. This technology became available after he had understood the secrets of inheritance; after he had understood (at least in the rough outline) the working of the genes and the DNA. Today, man is using genetic engineering to modify life or even create new life forms.

He can use this technology to improve the yield, to create cheap plants that can survive even in the toughest environmental conditions, and he can create plants that are immune to many vermin, in short: he can use the technology to improve the nutritional situation of the poor and help them to escape from hunger. But for some reasons he prefers to produce plants that are immune to pesticides which are sold to the rich.

One of the best-selling group of genetically modified organisms are plants that are resistant against the pesticide Roundup. The plants have been produced by Monsanto – and Roundup is produced by Monsanto as well. Isn't that a nice coincidence? And it explains why innovations to improve the situation of the poor by using genetic engineering got somewhat delayed.

Roundup is a very aggressive pesticide. It kills every plant. To make sure it didn't harm the useful plants, it had to be sprayed before the useful plants grew. The problem was that during this time-delay some weeds could grow again and reduce the yield. So the farmers were spraying huge amounts of Roundup to deplete the soil from any living cell before they sowed the useful plants.

As the useful plants are now resistant against Roundup, this pesticide can be sprayed during the growth phase of the useful plants, thus the farmers can reduce the amount of Roundup they need to kill the plants (as they don't have to turn the fields into a lifeless desert). In the end, using genetically modified plants, the farmers will save money.

This sounds like a bad business idea for Monsanto: After all, they are also selling Roundup. Now they would be selling less – and making less profit. But history showed us that Monsanto wasn't that stupid.

For nature is full of resources. One of these resources is natural selection which is still at work today. Natural selection means that plants will adapt. If bacteria are exposed to antibiotics, they will become immune against them. That's causing a lot of headache in medicine at the moment, because we have been administrating antibiotics even to healthy animals just in case, giving many possibilities for bacteria to become immune.

The same is happening to plants: If they are exposed to a certain poison all the time, they will develop some resistance against that poison. So the farmer will have to increase the dose of poison to kill the weeds. But the weeds are becoming stronger each year, and the farmer has to increase the deadly dose each year. It is a race man cannot win. There is only one winner: Monsanto (and companies with similar products). So in the end, using genetically modified organisms that were supposed to reduce the costs for the farmers led to increased costs for them. And the revenues of the companies rose to the skies. Roundup is one of the best-selling pesticides on the market.

But fooling the buyers of genetically modified organisms is only part of the story. Once the plants have been harvested, they will end up in the stomach of the consumers. And nobody really knows if genetically modified plants pose a health risk to consumers. Countries like the USA, where genetically modified life forms are sold, don't think there are risks, but this is more wishful thinking than hard science.

The authorities have simply decided that there is no risk to consumers, because genetically modified plants are "substantially equivalent" to their natural cousins. This means that genetically modified plants can mean no harm if the natural plants they have been derived from and the genetic code that was introduced in the plant have been harmless. For how could the mixture of two harmless things produce something harmful?

Maybe the authorities should ask their colleagues from the army. The military has been using this approach since decades to store chemical weapons. Creating the toxic substance and storing it could be problematic. There could always be leaks or other ways for the substance to escape and cause harm. So the army created "binary chemical weapons" that are using two harmless substances which are non-toxic for humans. Only when the weapon is used, these two harmless substances combine, creating deadly poisons like the sarin nerve gas.

Agreed, introducing a new DNA in an existing life form is not exactly like mixing two chemicals. But the result could be the same, for who can tell for sure how the new genetic code will behave? It could create any protein in its new environment. The authorities believe that this is not the case, but they never really bothered to conduct studies to find out. It seems to be self-evident. And those independent scientists who bothered to find out came up with unsettling answers: Genetically modified food might be more dangerous than we think. It can cause cancer and is treated as an invader by the human immune system.

But we keep on using the new products of our technology, nevertheless. They might do direct harm to us, and they do indirect harm to us as they lead to a high usage of pesticides that will end up on our plates. But we don't seem to care.

Genetic engineering was meant to improve our life and help the poor against the constant threat of hunger. But the questions about the safety of this technology have not been answered in a satisfying way, and the way we are using it is to create products whose only goal is to increase the revenues for some companies. The side-effects of the products, like an increased chemical burden in our environment caused by the higher usage of pesticides and possible direct harm to the consumers, is not discussed and doesn't seem to matter. We are acting as we always did in the past: We use a new technology and simply hope for the best.

Fight Technology with Technology

But sometimes hope isn't the best answer to solve a problem. You might try it with prayers, after all it is said that faith can move mountains, but as the mountains have been fairly stable over past centuries, there is either not much faith in the world – or there is not much truth in the saying. If there are problems with technology, you have to find another way to deal with them.

One solution could be that you stop using the technology. If the risks of genetic engineering are too high (or too unclear) we could stop it and go back to the tedious process of breeding. But let's pause for a moment and think of a new technology that doesn't have side-effects. If we think of power plants, cars or plastic: There have always been negative side-effects. We solve one problem only to create a new one. If we stopped using a technology once problems arise, we would probably be left with the technology of the stone-age. And even with this technology man was able to wipe out all bigger mammals on the American continent...

Everything man had done since having been driven out of Paradise had a negative impact on Mother Nature; man's first civilizations were founded in the fertile regions of the Middle East – and he managed to destroy this fertility and leave only deserts.

But who would like to live in the stone-age again? It wasn't really such a fine time as depicted in the Flintstone-TV-show. It was a time when people were in deep fear of Nature, when superstition reigned; people died young and had to survive long periods of hunger and deprivation.

Some might praise the "natural" lifestyle of ancient pre-civilization tribes. But this is an idealized view from a saturated world. Those still living in stone-age-like tribes do everything they can to change to a modern lifestyle.

Technology makes our life easier (it's even possible to program a TV recorder nowadays), it makes it safer. Life without technology wouldn't be life as we know it anymore.

So we have to find another way to deal with problems that have arisen from the use of technology. And it seems that there is only one solution: Use technology to solve the problems that have been caused by technology.

At least, this is the approach we are taking today. This can be seen, for example, in the fishing industry. In past times, the seas seemed to be overflowing with fish. You just had to take your boat and your fishing-rod or net, and you were sure to come home after a short time with enough to feed your family and friends. The amount of fish man could catch was limited by the equipment he had available.

Fish, however, is a very nutritious food. Without the ability to freeze fish and thus keep it fresh for weeks, fish was mainly consumed by people at the coasts. But today we have much more people on earth who would like to eat fish – and we have the ability to keep fish fresh for weeks, so everyone even in the center of the continents can eat fish whenever he wants. The demand for fish has increased significantly, so has the technology to catch them.

If you take your little boat today to catch fish and return home after a few hours, you will not have caught much. Most fish regions are empty of fish; the trawlers have to sail to the deep ocean to find the fish. They use sophisticated technologies like sonar and radar to track them down and catch them in nets that are covering vast areas underneath the sea. These floating factories still manage to catch enough fish to still our huge demand. But even these factories sometimes return with their belly only half-filled. Today, the amount of fish we can catch is limited by the amount of fish there is.

But man always finds a solution. Some ten years ago the fish industry was using codfish to produce the popular fish fingers. But overfishing brought the population of codfish close to extinction. So the industry moved on: Today they are using the Alaska Pollock to produce the fish fingers – as long as it will last. Tomorrow we might use another fish that's still available in large amounts.

If there is a problem caused by technology, we use an even more sophisticated technology to solve it, even if this approach only means replacing one problem by another.

One of these problems is our oil-supply. Our civilization depends on oil; some even say it's a drug: We need it to feed our cars, we use it – to some amount – to produce electricity, and oil is the basis for our modern chemical industry. Only some years ago, we thought that the terrible moment called "peak oil" would soon be reached – some even thought it had already been reached. Peak oil it the maximum of the worldwide oil production, after that it could only go down as old oil fields were depleted and new ones could no longer be found.

In the world after peak oil, the oil price would only go up, so would the costs to drive a car, and the cheap synthetic chemical products that we are using would be become luxury goods in the near future. Our whole world would change, as it is based on oil – and this basis was eroding.

Alternatives were investigated intensively like electric cars or natural substances to replace artificial plastics. But none of them really took off – mainly because the quality of these alternatives was so much worse than what we could reach with oil-based technologies (just think of charging your battery every 200 kilometers – traveling from across the USA).

But in the end, everything's well that ends well. Well, at least we got a grace period. Thanks to technology we can now extract the oil from the tar sand which is found in Canada. And there is even an advantage with getting your oil from the tar sand: You don't have to dig deep holes into the earth to get the oil out from deep below. The tar sand can be found only some meters below the surface. You only have to remove the upper crust, the trees, the top soil, all life that usually lives there, and already you have access to the precious tar sand.

Acknowledged, this approach leaves lifeless deserts behind, but that is something mankind got used to from the first civilizations it founded in the Middle East. And Nature will find a way to make these deserts inhabitable again. She always does. Man might leave deep scars behind, but hasn't been able to kill Mother Nature. At least not yet.

Tar sand, however, isn't the goldmine that will save the human race from an oil-free future (or at least postpone this horror for another generation). The real goldmine became accessible through a technology called "fracking". This process made oil-fields available to the human race that were thought to be out of reach forever.

Fracking makes it possible to collect the endless number of little drops of oil that are hidden in shale layers deep in the earth. You can't extract them with the traditional technology. But with fracking you pump water mixed with sand and chemicals under high pressure into the earth. The water will crack the rocks and release the oil.

A drop in a bucket might not be worth a word. But millions of them are a completely different story. Practically from one day to another, the available oil-supply increased significantly. Today, we don't talk about peak oil anymore. That's far away in the future. And the USA, which is using the fracking-technology extensively, might become a net exporter of oil in a few years – today they are importing large amounts of oil from the Middle East.

"Peak oil", the Damocles sword hanging over our heads, is now far away in the future. It will happen one day, but thanks to technology it will not happen today.

But the fracking technology is like any other technology man has used. It solved a problem – and created another. The chemicals that are used to crack the rocks underground are not really harmless (as far as we know – the industry keeps the recipe of the mixtures they are using secret, so we are only able to get a short glimpse on the real composition). Everyone believed that it would not really matter how dangerous the chemicals are, because they are used hundreds of meters underground – well below the top soil and ground water, so there would be no danger of contaminating our environment and in the end us (because we are still part of environment, in spite of all technology).

This estimation, however, was probably too optimistic. Even though it should not happen (like nuclear power plants should not explode) several wells in the USA have been contaminated already. Somehow the chemicals used during fracking have found their way into the ground water. And some scientists believe that the chemicals used in this process could be the cause for some mysterious deaths of fish in rivers nearby.

Fracking has solved the problem that we were running out of oil. But the price we are paying is an even higher contamination of our environment.

This contamination is not only due to the chemicals used during the extraction process. Fossil fuels like oil and natural gas (which is also extracted using the fracking process) are a source of carbon dioxide. The carbon dioxide of the fossil fuels had been removed from the atmosphere for eons, buried deep down underground. Now we add it to the atmosphere again, where it acts like a greenhouse gas that will increase the temperature on earth. To be more precise: It will increase the average temperature on earth. While it gets hotter in some places, it might even get colder in other places. The climate of the earth is changing.

Climate changes are nothing new. They happened regularly in the history of the earth. The difference is: This time it is happening much faster than in the past. Natural climate changes take millennia to happen. The man-made climate change happens in a few decades. Mother Nature will have a tough time adapting to it, so will we. But we still might come up with new technologies to find solutions for that...

The climate change is not the only side-effect of a higher level of carbon dioxide in the atmosphere. Some part of the carbon dioxide is absorbed by the waters of the oceans where it forms carbon acid. Carbon acid, like any acid, attacks chalk (that's why phosphates, also some kind of acid, were so effective as additives to detergents). The chalk structure of many small creatures living in the sea is destroyed by carbon acid. This does not only affect the splendid corals, but also the tiny plankton. But plankton is at the beginning of the food-chain of sea animals. Without plankton, there will be no fish who feed on them, without fish there will be…

Well, there will be humans. By then we probably have learned to genetically modify fish so that they can feed on grass or algae, or only love and air.

Genetic engineering might be the only solution that we have to adapt ourselves and the plants and animals we feed on to a quickly changing environment. Natural selection might have done this on its own if the climate were changing over thousands of years, but today it looks as if only vermin that happily caused strange diseases in the tropics profit from the climate change and move to the previously colder regions of Europe and North America.

If we also want to have human-friendly animals and plants surviving the climate change, we might have to interfere in the process of natural selection with our superior technology.

If only we knew what we are doing…

We Ignore the Consequences

How can we increase our knowledge about the world – for there seems to be a lot we don't know? The answer to this question that was given by intellectuals for a long time seemed convincing – that's probably the reason why it lasted for more than two thousand years and is still popular with many, although it has been proved wrong in the meantime.

But we have to be fair: The answer was provided by one of the greatest minds that ever lived: The great philosopher Plato.

If we want to learn something about the world, we have two possibilities to tackle the questions: We can use our senses and experience the world, or we can use our mind and think about it.

If asked, what would be the correct approach to learn something about the world, the most obvious answer would be to use our senses. After all it's with our eyes that we see and our ears that we hear. Our mind alone is blind and deaf. But that's the point when philosophy steps in and tells us that the most obvious answer doesn't have to be the correct answer.

Plato mentioned the risky side of relying on our senses when trying to learn something about our world, for our senses can be tricked. We all know some sophisticated compositions of color spots that make us believe that there is a color spot of a different color right in the center – although in fact the paper is simply white. And we know that two drawn lines can give the impression of being of different length – although their lengths are exactly identical. Our senses can be fooled – and they are still fooled even though we know that there is no colored spot in the center or that the lines are of identical length. We know the truth, yet we don't see it. So we cannot rely on our senses to learn something about the world.

This is the message that Plato gave us more than two thousand years ago. If we want to understand the world, we cannot rely on our senses; instead we have to rely on our mind. Only with clear thinking, we are able to see the truth, to "look" behind the curtain of hallucinations and illusions that we receive through our senses. The mind is our trustful companion when we want to understand the world. Plato called this kind of philosophy "dialectics"; it was later on called "metaphysics" (because the works of Aristotle covering this subject were ranged after his works about physics in a complete edition).

Plato explained the way that we see the world in his Allegory of the Cave. The Allegory is about some human beings that have been imprisoned in a special cave right from their birth. These prisoners are chained to the rocks and held immobile so that they can only gaze at a wall in front of them. Behind the prisoners, there is an enormous fire that projects everything that is happening between the fire and the prisoners onto the wall.

The prisoners cannot see the people walking behind them. They can only see their shadows on the wall, but they don't know that they are shadows. The prisoners think that they see the real world, the world as it is, for this is all they know about the world. So they take the shadows on the wall for the real creatures living on earth and the echoes off the wall for the real sound connected to the shadows.

These prisoners, Plato tells us, are we, when we only use our senses. We believe to experience the real world, but the real world is hidden from our views. We have to free ourselves (i.e. use our mind) to understand the real world.

And our mind will not fail us in this task, because it is the "divine spirit", the little godly part of us that makes us superior to animals and lifts us above the pure earthly things. How could this divine mind fool us if it was given to us by God? When our thinking is clear and logical, we will inevitably find the truth about the world.

This understanding of "science", of how man should try to understand the world, was not questioned for more than two thousand years. First doubts that the approach was not correct appeared in the 17th century, when scientists like Galileo Galilei simply chose experiments to find the laws of physics instead of relying on their thinking. But metaphysics was only openly challenged in the 18th century. The revolution in philosophy became the name "empiricism" and was based on the British island where scientist and engineers quietly started an industrial revolution by basing all their doings on experience – and not so much on thinking.

The most famous representative of empiricism was David Hume. He radically rejected any philosophical thought that was purely based on thinking. Metaphysics was idle talk to his understanding; it could bring up any idea and you could not know if it was correct. To decide this, you needed the experience. You couldn't decide what color a dog has just by thinking of it; you had to look at it to decide that question. But when you needed experience to decide which thought is right, then thinking as the basis of understanding the world is a pointless exercise in general. In a radical contradiction to Plato, who rejected experience and relied on thinking, Hume rejected thinking and relied purely on experience.

This means, that you can only make statements about the past and the present, because you have experienced these times (or are experiencing it right now). The future is completely unknown to you – and will always be unknown. When you think that you can predict the future based on mathematical theories, then you are wrong, because equations – which are nothing more than coded thinking – can't tell you anything about the world. They are nothing more than imaginations of the human mind. Thus his famous saying:

> "That the sun will not rise tomorrow is no
> less intelligible a proposition, and implies no
> more contradiction, than the affirmation,
> that it will rise."

We can only know that the sun will rise when we have experienced that is has risen. Everything else is just a figment of your imagination.

And our mind can imagine everything. It can come up with the idea that an apple will fall to the ground, and it can imagine that and apple will rise to the sky once its connection to the tree is lost – for how should we know that gravity prevails without having experienced it? Our mind can imagine that we will burn our hand if we hold it into a flame; and it can imagine that we will freeze our hand if we hold it into a flame – for how should we know that a flame is burning hot without having experienced it?

We will only know what will happen, if we use our senses and test it. Everything is possible in our minds.

The total rejection of our thinking and even declaring that we are not able to predict the sunrise, even though we were quite successful in the past (or just lucky?), seems to be exaggerated. And maybe Hume wasn't really serious about such a radical view (after all, with Englishmen and their sense of humor, you can never be sure). But Hume was definitely right when he stated that trying to understand something about the world just by thinking about it is a complete waste of time, because you can think of anything and will never know what's real in our world.

This argument, further elaborate by Immanuel Kant some years later, provides a deadly blow to metaphysics, which is the reason why it is not very popular among these "thinkers". But thanks to Hegel, the impossible became possible once more. Hegel simply stated that the incapability of pure reason to decide which thesis is correct is not a failure of metaphysics, but the way metaphysics works. Thesis and antithesis (you don't know which one is right) form a new synthesis that gives birth to another antithesis. Step by step, philosophy will evolve. It will never find an answer, though, as even after the millionths circle it will not be able to tell you if the thesis or the antithesis is correct (you are trapped in an endless circle), but at least it keeps philosophers busy and let's them earn some money paid by simpletons who never understood Hume's and Kant's critique.

Hume showed that thinking alone will tell us nothing about the world. He put his bets on experience alone, for you need it anyway to find out which idea is correct. Kant argued that experience alone doesn't help either. If you only collected experiences, you would just amass tons of information without any connection between them. You need your mind to put them in order, to bring some meaning to them. Only thinking and experiencing combined can help us to understand the world.

This may sound like Hegel's thesis plus antithesis generate a synthesis approach. But in the case of Kant, the story ends here and is not trapped in an endless circle.

The approach Kant was describing is the approach scientist had already been taking instinctively since more than a century: You collect data and then come up with a theory to explain them. Or you invent a theory and then make some experiments to confirm it – or to prove it wrong. Only the combination of theory and experiment, of thinking and experiencing will yield useful results. And science was showing that these results were really useful – and more successful than any results metaphysics had generated in more than two thousand years.

Hume was nevertheless right in one point: You can never be sure that a theory will be right. There is no "mathematical proof" that will show us if a certain physical law is correct. You can only assume that it will be correct unless proved otherwise. This is what happened to Newton's theory of gravitation which correctly describes the attraction of masses – until the masses become too heavy or move very fast (then Einstein's relativity applies) or until the masses become very small (then we have to use quantum mechanics).

This happened in other cases (like phlogiston, a substance that should leave an object when it was burned, now we know that burning objects forms bonds with the oxygen in the air), and it will happen again, because science is made by men, not by gods.

*

This short summary of the discussion between metaphysics and science explains why the technical progress often seems to replace one problem with another. We are not able to know the future: Metaphysics will tell us nothing, it is worthless and idle talk; and science can make some educated guesses, but scientist can never be sure. Their theories might be wrong and might lead us in a wrong direction. The future remains the "undiscovered country", and we can't know what's going on until we have seen it.

Our experiences in the past might give us a hint of what might happen. But we can't know for sure, because we cannot think of everything. During the Second World War, the USA gathered the most distinguished and established scientist in Los Alamos to build the atomic bomb, because the Americans feared that Nazi-Germany might be doing the same. Most of these scientists died of cancer. They were not aware of the dangers of radioactivity; otherwise they would have tried to protect their body better to avoid the contamination.

Monsanto started to sell a genetically modified corn plant some years ago. This plant was special as it produced a poison against the Western corn rootworm, a little insect that was heavily damaging the corn fields in the Midwest. It is also called the "one-billion-dollar-bug" as it caused such huge damages each year.

But the genetically modified corn of Monsanto was very successful. It managed to eradicate the Western corn rootworm in many areas. So everything would have been fine, the investment in the more expensive corn seeds of Monsanto would have been justified and the farmers could live happy ever after.

Unfortunately, Mother Nature is very imaginative and has large resources. Once the Western corn rootworm had disappeared, the Western bean cutworm took over the empty ecological niche and is now causing as much damages as the rootworm once did.

We are not able to foretell the future. We can only know for sure what will happen when we experience it. We are only smarter afterwards.

This is shown by a nice little scene about the famous physicist Enrico Fermi. He was one of the founders of quantum mechanics and the first to control a nuclear fission in his laboratory, in his prototype for nuclear reactors. Fermi was once addressed by a student who had observed that the number of neutrons would decrease in a certain experiment. "That", Fermi said, "can easily be explained." The student looked at his numbers and corrected himself: In fact, the number of neutrons increased in that experiment. "That", the great Fermi said without hesitation, "can even more easily be explained."

It is not by thinking that we will understand the world, only by experiencing it.

*

This essay is not meant to be a diatribe against technology. It was already mentioned in the beginning: We owe a lot to technology. I can't imagine that anyone would seriously consider exchanging his life today against a life in the Middle Ages, at least I wouldn't. We need science and technology. They made our lives easier and they freed us from the slavery of esotericism and religion, which simply pretend things and don't care to find out if they are really true – but show maximum intolerance if someone dares to contradict their teachings.

This is not meant to say that the prophets of the religions were liars. They might have been very well convinced of what they said. But how could they really know what an almighty and all-knowing God was telling them as they were only human and thus far from being almighty and all-knowing?

This is best illustrated by a story that is being told in the Buddhist culture: Let's imagine three blind men. They have to describe an elephant. The first one is touching the leg of the elephant and says: The elephant looks like a tree. The second one is touching the trunk of the elephant and says: The elephant looks like a snake. The third one is touching the side of the elephant and says: The elephant looks like a wall.

Just like the blind man can't know what an elephant really looks like (even if they figure out the correct form, the color will always be a mystery to them), no prophet can know for sure what God looks like and what he really wants, because his mind is so much bigger than ours and his sayings and actions can only be misinterpreted by man.

183

It's because of man's limited mind that religions have to be wrong. And it's because of the impossibility to experience God that all we know about him can only be myths. We will never be able to know the truth in religion, even though the prophets pretend to tell us the ultimate truth in their writings.

Science at least has the possibility to find the truth, as it doesn't only believe. It is not convinced that it knows the truth so it keeps on looking. This requires a tolerant mindset, because you have to accept that you can be wrong. Such an idea will never cross the mind of a dogmatic believer.

Science and technology thus prepared not only the ground for an improved quality of life, they also prepared the ground for a more human and democratic society. We simply can't do without them.

But we have to be careful how we handle modern technology. When man did his first technological inventions, they were rather simple. The fire, the wheel and the iron sword could do some harm, but they could never kill thousands of people.

The quality of our technology, however, has changed over time. Today our technology is powerful enough to destroy all human life. We have invented biological and chemical weapons that can kill thousands. We master (as good as we can) the atomic forces and build bombs than can destroy whole cities in the fraction of a second. And we conduct worldwide experiments by changing the climate and by releasing genetically modified organisms into the environment, while consequences are not known to us. We are acting like little children who are playing with dynamite but don't know anything about it. We might not be God, but we are very close to the Devil, if we don't pay attention.

We think that we can handle these powers. But we don't really know anything. So all we can do is to be careful with new technologies. We cannot just use them and then hope for the best. We have to make sure that they will do no harm – and even if we check this, there is some probability that we will miss something that causes new problems. But without checking first, we can be sure that we will only replace one problem with another – and that we will cause more harm than do good.

Believe in Religion – and be fooled

The Origin of Religion

Andy Warhol once said that in the future, everyone will be world-famous for 15 minutes. This was meant to describe the speed of our times, where we quickly lose interest in persons and situations and seem to have the attention span of newborn children. But it also was meant to show that thanks to the new media everyone could have the chance to become famous – even if it was only for a short time.

Some people, however, manage to stay famous. Andy Warhol's fame even didn't disappear after his death. The American president is known to many of us, Bono Vox, the singer of the rock-group U2, is another famous person, just like the physicist Albert Einstein, best remembered for the picture on which he stuck his tongue out on us.

But probably the most famous person, if we may call him that, is God. Nobody has ever seen him, nobody has ever taken a picture of him, but we all have a fairly good understanding of what he should look like: A benign old man with white hair and a white, long beard.

This brings up the question why an almighty, all-knowing and superhuman being should look like us, but of course the question attacks the problem from the wrong side. The Bible explicitly tells us, that God doesn't look like us (meaning that our appearance was the example for the looks of God), but that humans were created by God to his image. Humans look like God, not the other way round.

Nevertheless, some heretics have their doubts if this is really the true story. One of them was the Greek philosopher Xehophanes, who lived in the 5th century before Jesus Christ was born – which shows us that some questions are as old as mankind.

Xenophanes wrote a little poem, which reads:

> But if cattle and horses and lions had hands
> or could paint with their hands and create
> works such as men do,
>
> horses like horses and cattle like cattle
> also would depict the gods' shapes and
> make their bodies
>
> of such a sort as the form they themselves
> have.

Even before the Bible was written, some philosophers thought that God (or the gods in the case of the Greek) was created by humans. If you have a closer look at the Greek gods, you can understand that this is a valid question: They are jealous, vengeful, fall in love, hate each other and simply behave like any other group of humans would behave.

Maybe man did invent the gods. And why not, he had all the reasons to do so: Man is surrounded by an incomprehensible nature where thinks simply seem to be happening – but man doesn't like it when things simply happen. He wants to understand why; and any story that seems plausible enough will do in the times before science. So maybe man had invented the gods?

After all, the sun was going up each morning and moving over the sky, but what was the sun and who had put it up there? All of a sudden, a sunny day could turn into a wild thunderstorm, killing people with lighting – what had happened? Sometimes the weather was pleasant and let the plants grow, sometimes a hailstorm or a drought killed all the plants and left the people starving – why did this happen, what had they done?

The world was full of mysterious and incomprehensible behaviors. Biggest of all was the mystery how man had come on earth – how had man and all the animals and plants been created?

In pre-scientific times, the religion provided answers to all this and the stories were told from generation to generation to give a meaning to life. When the weather turned bad and destroyed the harvest, this meant that the gods were angry with man. Man had probably misbehaved and was punished for his actions. And some years ago, maybe in the year 4004 B.C. as the English theologian James Ussher had calculated in the 17th century, the world with all its inhabitants and all the stars and planets in the sky was created by God.

The religions, of course, deny that God was created by man. In their understanding, the creation happened as described in the Bible:

> In the beginning God created the heaven and the earth. And the earth was without form, and void; and darkness was upon the face of the deep. And the Spirit of God moved upon the face of the waters. And God said, Let there be light: and there was light. And God saw the light, that it was good: and God divided the light from the darkness. And God called the light Day, and the darkness he called Night. And the evening and the morning were the first day.
>
> And God said, Let there be a firmament in the midst of the waters, and let it divide the waters from the waters. And God made the firmament, and divided the waters which were under the firmament from the waters which were above the firmament: and it was so.   And God called the firmament

Heaven. And the evening and the morning were the second day.

And God said, Let the waters under the heaven be gathered together unto one place, and let the dry land appear: and it was so. And God called the dry land Earth; and the gathering together of the waters called the Seas: and God saw that it was good. And God said, Let the earth bring forth grass, the herb yielding seed, and the fruit tree yielding fruit after his kind, whose seed is in itself, upon the earth: and it was so. And the earth brought forth grass, and herb yielding seed after his kind, and the tree yielding fruit, whose seed was in itself, after his kind: and God saw that it was good. And the evening and the morning were the third day.

And God said, Let there be lights in the firmament of the heaven to divide the day from the night; and let them be for signs, and for seasons, and for days, and years: and let them be for lights in the firmament of the heaven to give light upon the earth: and it was so. And God made two great lights; the greater light to rule the day, and the lesser light to rule the night: he made the stars also. And God set them in the firmament of the heaven to give light upon the earth, and to rule over the day and over the night, and to divide the light from the darkness: and God saw that it was good. And the evening and the morning were the fourth day.

And God said, Let the waters bring forth abundantly the moving creature that hath life, and fowl that may fly above the earth in the open firmament of heaven. And God created great whales, and every living creature that moves, which the waters brought forth abundantly, after their kind, and every winged fowl after his kind: and God saw that it was good. And God blessed them, saying, Be fruitful, and multiply, and fill the waters in the seas, and let fowl multiply in the earth. And the evening and the morning were the fifth day.

And God said, Let the earth bring forth the living creature after his kind, cattle, and creeping thing, and beast of the earth after his kind: and it was so. And God made the beast of the earth after his kind, and cattle after their kind, and everything that creeps upon the earth after his kind: and God saw that it was good. And God said, Let us make man in our image, after our likeness: and let them have dominion over the fish of the sea, and over the fowl of the air, and over the cattle, and over all the earth, and over every creeping thing that creeps upon the earth. So God created man in his own image, in the image of God created he him; male and female created he them. And God blessed them, and God said unto them, Be fruitful, and multiply, and replenish the earth, and subdue it: and have dominion over the fish of the sea, and over the fowl of the air, and over every living thing that moves upon the earth. And God said, Behold, I have given you every herb bearing seed, which is upon the face of all the earth, and every tree, in the which is the fruit of a tree yielding seed; to you it shall be for meat. And to every beast of the earth, and to every fowl of the air, and to everything that creeps upon the earth, wherein there is life, I have given every green herb for meat: and it was so. And God saw everything that he had made, and, behold, it was very good. And the evening and the morning were the sixth day.

This is the official version of the Creation. According to the believers, this is how the earth was created. You might argue if a day is really a day with twenty-four hours or only means a not well defined period of time, but that's the whole concession the believers of the true faith will make. Religion is not man-made; the holy books tell us what really happened.

The problem is only: There are so many of stories of creation out there. The Greek and the Egyptian people have completely different stories of how the world was made.

The Egyptians believed that the first god, Atum, created himself and left the waters of "Nun" which covered the earth. Land appeared at the very spot that Atum had left the waters of Nun. He spat his son, the god of the airs Schu, and vomited his daughter, the god of humidity Tefnut. One day, his children left him, and Atum cried bitter tears which formed the first human beings.

According to the Greek, it was Prometheus who got the order from the other Gods to create man from earth and water. He did this, but abused his powers to steal Athena's wisdom and the fire from Hephaestus and gave both to man. The Gods punished Prometheus by chaining him to a rock, and an eagle would appear each day to eat his liver which would recover over night.

The stories of the Greek and the Egyptians are very far away from what we consider today to be the true story of evolution, i.e. the earth was created first, then the plants and animals and finally man. The creation described in the Bible comes strangely close to that sequence. So maybe it is the correct description of the Creation and the Old Testament, the basis for religions like Christianity, Judaism, and Islam, tells the only truth about the Creation?

It is astonishing, but not even the Bible seems to be sure what should be the correct description of the Creation. Some pages later, we read the following account:

> These are the generations of the heavens and of the earth when they were created, in the day that the Lord God made the earth and the heavens, and every plant of the field before it was in the earth, and every herb of the field before it grew: for the Lord God had not caused it to rain upon the earth, and there was not a man to till the ground.
>
> But there went up a mist from the earth, and watered the whole face of the ground. And the Lord God formed man of the dust of the ground, and breathed into his nostrils the breath of life; and man became a living soul.
>
> And the Lord God planted a garden eastward in Eden; and there he put the man whom he had formed. And out of the ground made the Lord God to grow every tree that is pleasant to the sight, and good

for food; the tree of life also in the midst of the garden, and the tree of knowledge of good and evil.

And a river went out of Eden to water the garden; and from thence it was parted, and became into four heads. The name of the first is Pison: that is it which compasses the whole land of Hav'ilah, where there is gold; and the gold of that land is good: there is bdellium and the onyx stone. And the name of the second river is Gihon: the same is it that compasses the whole land of Ethiopia. And the name of the third river is Hid'dekel: that is it which goes toward the east of Assyria. And the fourth river is Euphra'tes.

And the Lord God took the man, and put him into the garden of Eden to dress it and to keep it. And the Lord God commanded the man, saying, Of every tree of the garden thou may freely eat: but of the tree of the knowledge of good and evil, thou shall not eat of it: for in the day that thou eat thereof you shall surely die.

And the Lord God said, It is not good that the man should be alone; I will make him a help meet for him. And out of the ground the Lord God formed every beast of the field, and every fowl of the air; and brought them unto Adam to see what he would call them: and whatsoever Adam called every living creature, that was the name thereof. And Adam gave names to all cattle, and to the fowl of the air, and to every beast of the field; but for Adam there was not found a help meet for him. And the Lord God caused a deep sleep to fall upon Adam, and he slept; and he took one of his ribs, and closed up the flesh instead thereof.   And the rib, which the Lord God had taken from man, made he a woman, and brought her unto the man. And Adam said, This is now bone of my bones, and flesh of my flesh: she shall be called Woman, because she was taken out of Man.

This time, the order is reversed: Man was created first (well, the male part of the human race, but that's all that counts in most religions) and then the plants and animals. Just some pages later, the Bible contradicts itself and presents a completely different story of creation. Which one is correct?

We can find several contradicting statements in the Bible. In the Old Testament, God is described as an irascible person. His motto is "an eye for an eye", whereas it changes completely to "But I tell you, do not resist an evil person. If anyone slaps you on the right cheek, turn to them the other cheek also" in the New Testament.

The religion pretends that their holy books have been inspired or even written by God directly. If this were the case, why do we have all these contradictions in the text?

Humans are prone to errors. Errar humanum est, it's human to err, as the Romans said. Maybe the religions have been invented by humans, after all, and that is the reason why we have these contradictions in the holy texts.

But maybe these questions are not really important, because we need a religion, no matter how they came into our lives. After all, religions are moral institutions

The Moral of Religion

Talk-Shows are very popular on television nowadays. They have one big advantage: They are cheap to produce. You can fill hours with people taking, and people like to watch other people talking. Either because it is interesting or because it is so embarrassing that it also gets kind of interesting.

There seems to be a general rule when it comes to talk-shows: Whenever people are talking about moral, you have to invite a priest, a monk or a theologian. This seems to be a general rule in our world: Even when governments try to solve moral problems, they invite clerics to join the commission who will discuss the problem (the commissions don't necessarily solve the problem, but at least they give the impression that the government is doing something).

It seems that the church, that the religion is considered to be an important institution when it comes to moral behavior. That is also what religions are advertising about themselves. They know the real good, after all they are acting in the name of God (let's forget about the handful of Satanists for the moment) and God is the absolute Good.

God even gave us moral rules like the Ten Commandments that shall guide our lives. "Thou shalt not kill" and "thou shalt not steal" are orders that we still accept, more than 2000 years after they have been written down. And each Sunday the priests are telling us how important a moral behavior is – and what it should look like. Okay, in our days we don't necessarily agree with everything the church is telling us. Abortion is not considered immoral under certain circumstances, and the wife is no longer the slave to her husband as this used to be. But even though we disagree in details, in general we accept the self-given statement of the churches that they are the caretakers of morality.

There are just two problems with this statement. The first problem is that religion relies on God for its morality. The prophets of the religion claim that they received the holy words they had written down or had communicated directly from God. This statement is not supported by an independent observation as this is required from science, where everyone can see that all things fall down to earth, which strongly supports the idea of gravity. In the case of religion, we simply have to believe the words of the prophets that their statements and the rules mentioned in the statements have been given to them by God. But let us assume that the prophets are telling the truth (you see: Religion is not really about believing in God, it is rather about believing in the prophets), let us assume that the prophets were not victims to some hallucinations, but that they really heard the voice of God and received instructions from him.

Then we only have one problem: Can we be sure that the prophets understood God correctly? After all, God is almighty and all-knowing. He has a mind that surpasses ours by several orders of magnitude. We even have problems to understand a human scientist when he is talking about his scientific expertise like the theory of general relativity or derivatives in banking. How should a human being be able to understand a superhuman being whose mind is so much bigger than ours that our minds must appear to God as the minds of mice would appear to us?

Even if we assume that God was talking directly to the prophets, it is very unlikely that they understood him correctly. They rather acted like the famous blind men who had to describe an elephant.

As the blind men couldn't see the elephant, they were using their hands to get an "image" of his body. The first one was touching the leg of the elephant and said: The elephant looks like a tree. The second one was touching the trunk of the elephant and said: The elephant looks like a snake. The third one was touching the side of the elephant and said: The elephant looks like a wall.

All three men have described correctly what they "saw". Only the elephant was so much bigger that they were not able to "see" everything. And even if they had been able to describe the elephant's body correctly, they would never be able to describe his color. This is simply beyond their abilities, just like it is beyond the abilities of human being's to understand the superhuman mind of God.

If we have to assume, that God's rules have been incorrectly delivered by the prophets, then we also have to assume that their moral rules are not really the moral rules of God. So why should they be superior to any other set of moral rules?

*

The second reason why we have to doubt that religion is really the caretaker of morality is due to its behavior.

Morality tells us what is good and what is wrong. But we also judge the process of decision according to our moral values. If the judge shows no mercy and ruthlessly condemns those that trespassed against the limits set by the rules, then we have doubts about the morality of the judge himself.

Humans are empathic beings. When someone suffers, we suffer with him, when someone is joyful, we rejoice with him. Strictly following rules and handing out punishments if they are only slightly bend without considering the circumstances, without considering the personality of the wrongdoer is heartless. This could be done by a machine, but it is not a human behavior. We expect empathy, and we expect tolerance. Any set of moral rules should allow for some tolerance, it should provide some freedom to speak your mind and contradict others; it should provide the individual human rights.

This, however, is something religion cannot provide. Religion pretends and believes to be in the possession of the absolute truth. Its truth is the only right and good truth. Any contradicting opinion is wrong, if not inspired by the enemies of the religion, by Satan himself. Religion has to be intolerant; it has to suppress human rights.

It cannot treat dissidents as equals, for this would give the impression that their opinion could also be true. Even more: dissidents could gain more partisans and one day they could outnumber the believers of the true faith, threatening the further survival of the religion. Any religion who thinks that it is worthy to survive, that believes to be in the possession of the only truth (and which religion doesn't) has to assure that such a development will never happen. Religion has to get rid of dissidents as soon as they appear.

And that is what every religion did. Just have a look at the religion we are most familiar with: Christianity.

The Christian belief is based on the Revelations that can be read in the Bible. We already mentioned the example of the story of Creation where the Bible even contradicts itself and doesn't need a third party as an opposition. But true believers don't care. "I believe because it is absurd", as Tertullian, one of the church fathers, said in the second century A.C. And so the Christians believed and didn't bother to know – and Europe fell back in time. The Europeans forgot everything about Science and Technology the Ancients had developed, and the buildings from Roman times looked like monuments from times when the gods live in earth (only the people were not allowed to believe in the gods, as there was only one and he never lived on earth).

The Islam showed a similar development. When Persia was conquered by the armies of the caliph in the 7th century, many scientific books fell in the hands of the Muslims. The caliph was asked if the books could be distributed among the soldiers, but he didn't see any necessity that anyone should read anything but the Koran. "If they contain the truth, the Koran as provided by God is a better guide. If they contradict the Koran, they contain lies. In both cases, the books should be destroyed."

There is only one truth in religion: The religious leaders who believe to speak in the name of God can't be wrong.

And if we read in the Book of Joshua that Joshua commanded the sun to stand still in the sky (which it did, according to the Bible), this can only mean that the sun is moving around the earth (for how could the sun stand still if it didn't move?). So the Catholic Church was sure that the earth was in the center of the world (after all that was the place God had chosen to create man and his female sidekick) and everything else including the sun was moving around the earth.

The problem was that seen from earth the planets were moving on strange paths around the earth that could not easily be explained. Everything was much simpler if you assumed that the sun was in the center and the earth and all the other planets were moving around the sun, as Nicolaus Copernicus had proposed. But the Church was firm in its belief: everything up in the skies was moving around the earth.

This belief was shaken when Galileo Galilei discovered the moons of Jupiter. They were clearly moving around another planet and not the earth. So the fundamental truth that everything was moving around the earth was obviously wrong. Therefore, Galileo supported the model of the solar system as proposed by Copernicus.

But basing the belief on observation and experiment is not among your strengths if you believe in an invisible and yet almighty God. So the Church made it clear to Galileo: He either openly declared that his teaching that everything was moving around the sun was wrong – then he could live under house arrest for the rest of his live – or he could stand by his words and on a pyre which would be set in flames immediately. This wasn't really a choice, so Galileo openly admitted his mistakes and was allowed to live. It took more than 350 years that the Church admitted it had made a mistake and rehabilitated Galileo in the year 1992.

You cannot judge this change of mind high enough: Acknowledging that Galileo was right was a big step for an institution that believes to be in the possession of the absolute truth i.e. that believes it can't be wrong. For if you cannot be wrong, there is no need for you to be tolerant.

This is what happened to anyone who didn't share the opinion of the religion. Disbelievers like the Cathars, a Christian group that live up to the 13th century mainly in the south of France, was completely erased from earth only because they had a different understanding than the Catholic Church of what the Christian religion should look like.

Other disbelievers were put to trial and burnt on the stake. The trial was not really meant to find out if the accused was innocent or guilty as trials do today (or are suppose to do). If someone was accused by the inquisition, the inquisition had a good reason to do so, i.e. it knew that the accused was guilty (after all, they did God's work on earth, so they couldn't be wrong). The task of the inquisition was thus only to find the proof of his guilt – or get a confession of his guilt. And getting a confession was easy: With a little bit of torture, you can get any confession you want, and justice could be done (but we shouldn't think that torturing the accused was an easy task: The Pope had made it clear when permitting the use of torture that no blood should be spilled. It required quite some sensibility from the torturer to make sure that this didn't happen).

Everything was allowed in the religious fight against the disbelievers. After all, they were the enemy. That the religion, the Christian religion in Europe at least, is not so aggressive in its behavior anymore, may be due to the special situation in Europe: The states are secular, the church has lost its powers. It was different in times when the church was much more powerful (and human rights were unknown), and it is still the case in some Islamic states (and some say in the USA) where religious movements are much more powerful or are even the dominant power in the state. Disbelievers can easily be punished in such countries or even be convicted to death only because they have written something that the religious leaders consider being profane – as it happened to the writer Salman Rushdie who was condemned to death by the late religious leader of the Iran Ayatollah Khomeini.

Some are so stubborn in their religious belief and the ignorance of reality that they are even willing to kill themselves for the Higher Good – and take some of the devilish disbelievers with them. In general, you will not go to Heaven if you committed suicide. But these persons believe, because they committed suicide to kill disbelievers, that they will not only go to Heaven but be rewarded with 72 virgins that wait for them in Heaven. If the prophets and clerics, who do not show any intention of committing suicide for the higher cause themselves, got it right...

That's the main point in religion: You have to believe. If it contradicts you observations: You have to believe. If it contradicts common sense: You have to believe. But you do not believe in God, you have to believe his prophets. You have to believe that they got it right and transmitted the message correctly and didn't modify it to better suit their personal interests.

Science, on the other hand, isn't based on belief. Things are not necessarily correct because an authority tells you they have to be correct. You check on your own if they are correct. Science needs an open society; science supports democracy and tolerance because nobody is in the possession of the absolute truth.

Science is the opposite of religion. Science is the nemesis of religion, its biggest enemy.

And religion is willing to take on the fight.

Science is the Enemy of Religion

What is probably the worst thing that can happen to someone who absolutely believes he is right? The answer is simple: Prove him wrong. If you are convinced that you are in the possession of the only truth and someone tells you that your "truth" is wrong, your whole world shatters. The problem is not only that you have to acknowledge that you are wrong – which can be tough for your ego – the problem is even more dramatic: Others might not trust you anymore, as you proved to be unreliable, although quite convincing. And that can be even worse for your ego.

The magic of religion is that it demands absolute respect and absolute trust. Speaking in the name of God and pretending to act in His name, religion can ask for such loyalty and unquestioning obedience. But religion loses its magic touch if it is no longer *the* belief, but just one belief of many; if you can no longer put your trust in religion, because it might be proved wrong tomorrow like any other opinion.

Religion can only be a religion if nobody puts it in question. But that is exactly what science is doing.

Many statements thought to be eternal truths because they were written down in the Holy Books proved to be wrong. The earth is actually moving around the sun, even if you can find contradicting statements in the Bible. And the earth is about five million years old – and definitely much older than the 6000 years that was calculated based on dates given in the Bible. The statements of religion are no longer eternal truths, but just opinions. And like any other opinion, they can be wrong. So what's left there to believe in?

Science even goes one step further: The Bible, like any other religion, tells us that all animals and all plants and, probably most important, man has been created by God (even though the Bible can't agree on the order in which the Creation happened). But science tells us that the animals haven't been created once and lived since this time happily ever after. Science found evidence that some animals got extinct over time (which could still be aligned with the statement that all animals were created in one act of Creation by God, although you might wonder why the all-knowing being would take the effort of creating them in the first place if they wouldn't survive), and that new animals appeared long after the first animals disappeared from the face of the earth (which definitely can't be aligned with one act of Creation).

Even more: Laplace once wrote a book about the universe, the stars, the sun and the movements of the planets.

Napoleon had read the book and found one thing astonishing. So he asked Laplace why he didn't even mention God once when writing about the universe. Laplace's answer is legendary: "I didn't need this hypothesis."

You don't need divine actions to explain the movements of the planets in the sky, and you don't need divine action to explain the evolution of life on earth. But then: What's left for God?

Science puts a big question mark behind God's existence. There is no way to prove that God exists (Kant made this clear in his milestone-book "The Critique of Pure Reason"), and there is nothing left where we would need him to explain something. If there is a God, he is jobless by now.

Such an understanding undermines the authority of religion, so religion can't accept it. And religion fights back. As this is the case for any life-or-death struggle, religion doesn't really pay attention to its own rules. In their fight against science, religion breaks its own laws: "You shall not bear false witness against your neighbor."

As religion cannot refute the arguments of science, it simply tries to undermine its authority by spreading lies.

*

One battlefield of religion against science is the theory of evolution. If this theory is right, then there is no hide-out left for God. If evolution is correct, then we don't need a God to explain our existence. So religious believers came up with the "Theory of Intelligent Design" (formerly known as creationism) which claims that the theory of evolution is wrong and you need an "intelligence" (a.k.a. God) to explain life on earth.

Their first line of attack is the statement, that the theory of evolution is "just" a theory. It is not the absolute truth, so it is not fair that our children only hear about evolution at school but not about the "theory of intelligent design". Omitting the "theory of intelligent design" in the school books is nothing but censorship, which is illegal in all Western countries. The kids should have the possibility to choose for themselves which theory is right, just like they have the possibility to choose a political party during the elections.

This proposal sounds like a fair and democratic approach. But it only shows how perfidious the supporters of the "theory of intelligent design" are.

First of all: Science is not an electoral event. You cannot vote for what you like best, like having gravity today and removing it tomorrow or explaining the universe with the model of the Bible (the earth is in the center) today and tomorrow with Copernicus' model (the sun is in the center). What's right or wrong in science is decided by experiments, not by public vote.

But then: Evolution is "just" a theory, isn't it?

No, it isn't "just" a theory, and the supporters of "intelligent design" know this very well, because they hear it every time they bring up this argument – they just don't think they should change their arguments because it can fool those who are not so familiar with scientific terms.

If you come up with an idea to explain certain observations and facts, then scientists call this idea a "hypothesis". This hypothesis is tested again and again. And only if it has proved to be correct and no evidence could be found that it is wrong, then it is ennobled and called a "theory". The theory of evolution, therefore, is not "only" a theory; it is a proven explanation for thousands of data and has stood the test of time. The "theory" of intelligent design, however, is only a hypothesis and only called "theory" by its supporters as they try to confuse the people.

When you have broken through the lies that the supporters of "intelligent design" have come up with as a first line of attack against science, the supporters of "intelligent design" come up with other arguments. These arguments are not meant to prove that their "theory of intelligent design" is correct, but these arguments are meant to show that the theory of evolution is wrong. The basic argumentation is like this: Once they have shown that the theory of evolution is wrong, the "theory of intelligent design" has to be right. The supporters of this theory are so single-minded and arrogant that they don't see the possibility that there could be other theories that could be equally good explanations of existence of life on earth – like the Creation-"theory" the Egyptians came up with or the evolution theory of Lamarck (who thought that changes in the body are inherited from the parents to the children, giraffes thus developed a long neck as they tried to reach high-hanging leaves on trees, a feature which they inherited to their offspring).

These religious believers already have a hard time understanding that there is *one* opponent questioning their holy beliefs, they simply can't imagine that there could be more.

Even though the approach chosen by the supporters of "intelligent design" is pointless as it cannot show that their "theory" is correct, it is quite instructive to look at some of their arguments, as they keep on repeating them even though they should know by know that they are completely wrong. But they are at war with science, and at war, the truth dies first.

One popular statement of „intelligent design" is that evolution theory is in contradiction to one of the basic laws physics. They are referring to the laws of thermodynamics. The second law of thermodynamics states that "Heat cannot spontaneously flow from a colder location to a hotter location". Another way to express this is that entropy can never decrease in a closed system.

The entropy is a measure for disorder of a system. Just take the example of two containers with gas. As long as the two containers are separate, the system is well ordered: One gas is in the first container, the other gas is in the second container. Now let's remove the wall between these two containers. What will happen?

That's easy to predict: The gas molecules will mix. As the wall has been removed, there is no barrier anymore that would stop the molecules from moving into the other container. After some while, there will be gas molecules of both kinds in both containers. The disorder is at maximum, the entropy has increased.

The entropy provides us some sort of timeline. If you see a cup of coffee on the table in one picture and a broken cup on the floor surrounded by a puddle of coffee, and if you are asked, which picture has been taken first, you will never assumed that it is the second one. It is quite improbable that a broken cup will mend itself and move back onto the table. Assuming that someone touched the cup and it fell to the floor where it broke is more likely. The disorder increases, the entropy increases.

That's why heat is moving from hot to cold places and not the other way. Heat is a measure for the movement of the tiny particles, the atoms and molecules that we are consisting of. The faster they are moving, the hotter an object is, the higher is its entropy. If heat would be moving from hot to cold, then the entropy would decrease, which is not possible.

The statement that heat cannot move from hot to cold is the reason why there cannot be something like a perpetuum mobile. A perpetuum mobile is a machine that continues to move for ever after it has been started. In general, all machines stop after some time due to friction: Some part of the energy that was transferred to them to work is turned into heat, and after some time, there is not enough energy left to move the machine. A perpetuum mobile would be able to somehow turn this heat back into mechanical energy, so that it can still be used to drive the machine. The patent offices all around the world still receive applications for perpetuum mobiles, but they reject them without performing a proper search only based on the validity of the second law of thermodynamics.

When we now apply the second law of thermodynamics to evolution, we seem to have found a contradiction. What is the basic statement of evolution? Atoms were swimming around in the primeval ocean, completely disordered i.e. with high entropy, and then all of a sudden the miracle happened and the atoms formed molecules which finally formed such complicated life forms as human beings. The process of evolution is a process where entropy decreases. But this would be in contradiction to the second law of thermodynamics. Therefore, the theory of evolution has to be wrong.

The most remarkable feat about this argument is not the seemingly obvious conclusion, but the fact that the supporters of "intelligent design" keep on repeating it even though they have been told thousands of times that the argument is wrong. But we are at war, so there is no room for the truth.

The problem with the argument of "intelligent design" is that they ignore the few words "in a closed system". Entropy can never decrease in a closed system. The law doesn't say anything about an open system, anything could happen here.

A closed system is really a closed system. It is a well defined environment which is separated from the rest of the world, like the two containers. The gasses will be mixed for the rest of the time; there is no way they could be separated again. But let's assume someone has a very fine sorting machine that can grab the gas molecules and take them back to one container. Would this be possible or would it contradict the second law of thermodynamics?

Well, of course it would be possible, because now your closed system is no longer the two containers, but the two containers plus the sorting machine. The sorting machine will create heat while working. While it reduces the entropy in the two containers, it increases the entropy in its environment by heating it up. In the end, the overall entropy of the whole system will have increase, even though it has increased in the two boxes. But again, thermodynamics only make a statement about the behavior of entropy in the whole, closed system.

The situation is similar with evolution on earth. If earth were a closed system, the creation of life might have been unlikely, as it decreases the entropy significantly. It would need a very strong energy source that provides a lot of energy to balance this loss of entropy.

But earth isn't a closed system, and we have such an energy source: The sun. The sun is providing so much energy, that we could solve our energy problems today if we were able (and if we were willing) to convert just a tiny fraction of its energy into electricity. The sun is creating a lot of entropy, much more entropy than the evolution of life needs. In the closed system of our solar system, entropy is increasing even though life developed on the tiny blue planet moving around the sun (it really is moving around the sun, I am terribly sorry for the defenders of creationism).

This makes the most striking argument against evolution invalid – but as it is the most convincing argument, as it takes physics into the witness box, the supporters of "intelligent design" still use it. After all, scientist should be depicted as unreliable idiots, who don't even know their own laws!

When it comes to "intelligent design", scientists are not only idiots with regards to thermodynamics. Do you know how they find out the age of rocks in a certain rock strata? They use the fossils they find in there to tell them, because according to evolutionists, some animals only live during certain periods of time.

And do you know how they determine the age of the fossils? That's simple: They have a look at the rock strata they found it in, because certain fossils can only be found in certain strata.

The good thing is that scientist will never find a contradiction in this circular argument. But does this give the impression that science is reliable and knows what it is doing?

The way the supporters of "intelligent design" are telling the story: No. But again: They are not really telling the truth. This would ruin the punch-line. And did I mention that religion is at war with science?

The truth is less entertaining: Scientist first determine the age of a stratum. This can be done with the help of radioactive decay. You just measure how much of a certain radioactive material has decayed, and as you know the radioactive half-life of each element, you can quickly calculate the age of a certain rock. If you find a fossil in this rock stratum, you can safely assume that is has the same age, at least it would be difficult to explain how the rock should have formed first and the fossil in it later.

In if you have gathered enough information and are quite sure that one animal only lived in a certain, well-defined period in our past, then you can take fossils found in it to determine the age of strata, but only then.

I must admit that the scientific truth sounds much more boring and less entertaining than the story the supporters of "intelligent design" invented, but if you are talking science you shouldn't behave like in a political debate (unless you have absolute no clue what science is all about, that is).

Before we ask the supporters of the "intelligent design" how they explain our world, there is one more example the supporters of "intelligent design" have come up with to prove evolution wrong. It is called the "problem of irreducibility".

The examples starts with the observation that many parts of our body are quite complex. Just look at the eye: You have a lens that can change its focal point to have a sharp view on objects in different distances; on the retina you have small cells that only react to a certain color and other cells that only react to the brightness; and these different color and brightness information are then somehow combined in our brain to produce a picture of the world around us. It is simply impossible that such a complex organ like the eye could have appeared "out of nowhere" in the process of evolution.

Unfortunately (for the supporters of "intelligent design") nobody claimed that the eye appeared all of a sudden in the process of evolution. Instead, biologists have found dozens of tiny steps that show how the eye evolved from some simple light sensing cells on the skin to the complex organ that humans are using to see.

But the supporters of "intelligent design" are convinced that there are examples of parts of our body (or of the body of animals) that are so complex that they could not have appeared out of nowhere and where no intermediate steps can be found that would lead to the organ. In short, this organ would be irreducible, and the "problem of irreducibility" would prove evolution wrong.

The supporters of "intelligent design" had to look quite a while for an example, but they finally found something, when they looked at protozoa. These tiny animals only consist of one cell, but many of them have flagella, little organs that look like whips and are used to move the cells forward. They are the "legs" of bacteria, so to say, although they rather work like a little propeller, pushing the protozoa forward.

If only one protein forming the flagella was missing, it wouldn't work properly. And the flagella consists of forty different proteins. The probability that these proteins spontaneously came together to form the flagella is negligible. This would never have happened. And it means that we need an intelligent designer to explain the existence of flagella.

As most of the stories the supporters of "intelligent design" are telling, this one is again incomplete. Maybe nobody was able to come up with some intermediate step between nothing and the final flagellum in the first place, but if science doesn't have an answer yet doesn't mean there is none. Only someone believing in an absolute truth (and nothing else out there) could come up with such an argument.

And in the meantime, biologists have found an intermediate step. Some bacteria have a needle-like structure that is used to inject poison into other cells. This structure is very simple – and is also the core building block of a flagellum. An incomplete flagellum might not be used as a means for motion, but it can be used otherwise.

The argumentation of supporters of the "intelligent design" tries to build on the still incomplete understanding that we have about our world. We are not God, so we cannot know everything; there will always be some white spots behind which God could be hiding. But each time religious people tell us that God is the explanation, it only takes some time to figure out that this "hypothesis" (as Laplace put it) isn't needed.

Thunder is not made by a God, nor is it a God who causes wars or let's our plants grow. All this has secular explanations where the hypothesis God is not needed. But if religious people got the power of God wrong that often – how can we be sure that they are right this time, and the white spot on our understanding of the world is really the hiding place of the Almighty?

Let us turn the game around and ask the supporters of the "intelligent design", who want to make us believe that the Bible contains the only correct statements about the world, how they explain our world, the existence of man and the fossils?

We already mentioned that the Bible tells us that the sun is moving around the world. The people of ancient times didn't know this better, but a God should have known that this is wrong. Maybe he tried to tell the prophets, but they didn't understand this correctly. If they made a mistake here – where else did they misunderstand the Lord?

If we ask religious people what happened during Creation, they usually tell us about the first story of Creation where God created man in six days. This is a nice story, as it roughly fits to the findings of evolution. However, the second story, where man was created first and then the rest of the world, is generally ignored. But if the Bible is always right – how can we have two contradicting stories?

And if the Bible gives us a complete account of everything that has happened between the creation of the world and the death of God's son, then the earth should only be about six thousand years old (it was calculated that creation happened in the year 4004 B.C.). There are hundreds of proofs that this isn't the case. Earth has to be much older. Geology, the moving of continents, is a very slow process. If we find traces of old seas up in the mountains, then this means the geologic processes put the former sea ground in heights of several thousand meters. This takes millions of years, and not just a few hundred years.

But maybe, the supporters of "intelligent design" tell us, it wasn't necessary that the sea ground moved up. Remember the Deluge? The whole earth was covered by water. It was not necessary that the sea ground moves up to the mountains, as the water was covering the mountains. And the Deluge, by the way, also explains all the fossils: These animals simply died during the Deluge; they drowned. And the Deluge can even explain more: We see that more simply life forms are found in deeper rock strata, in the older strata. That's because the more simple life forms are less intelligent and were thus less able to survive. They died first when confronted with the insurmountable task to survive during the Deluge. See, we don't need millions of years and evolution to explain the fossils. But without them: What's left about evolution?

Let's go one step back. The reason for the Deluge was that God was not happy with his Creation:

> "And the Lord saw that the wickedness of man was great in the earth, and that every imagination of the thoughts of his heart was only evil continually.

> And it repented the Lord that He had made
> man on the earth, and it grieved Him at His
> heart."

So God made the decision to destroy his creation (it makes you wonder why the all-knowing God didn't know before that his Creation would turn out to be evil – but logic isn't the strength of a religion that you have to believe because it's absurd). But he had pity with Noah and his family, because they had been righteous and whole-hearted for generations. God therefore asked Noah to build an ark big enough for Noah and his family.

> "And of every living thing of all flesh, two
> of every sort shalt thou bring into the ark, to
> keep them alive with thee; they shall be male
> and female."

As Noah had two of every kind on his ark, we might wonder why some animals finally died out during the Deluge. But the story is even more confusing. God gave Noah concrete orders what the ark should look like:

> "And this is how thou shalt make it: the
> length of the ark three hundred cubits, the
> breadth of it fifty cubits, and the height of it
> thirty cubits."

A cubit is about half a meter, which means that the ark had a size of a football field. It furthermore had three levels, so Noah had the size of three football fields at his disposal to save all animals. This seems to be a lot, but if you think of all the different kind of animals living in the world, you can see that it is, in fact, nothing.

That might explain why some animals got extinct after the Deluge: There simply was no room for them on the ark. But even the animals that survived would never have fit on the ark. Unless they evolved after the Deluge – but that is a thought which cannot be thought.

The story of the Deluge tells us about a God who explicitly wants all animals to be saved (at least two of them) and then orders Noah to build an ark which is too small for this task. Either God didn't know what he wanted to achieve, or the prophets misunderstood him. In both cases, the Bible isn't really a reliable source to understand the beginning of our existence.

And by the way: Even if the supporters of "intelligent design" were right and the stupid animals died first during the Deluge: The fossil record shows us that fish are among the oldest animals on our world. They died first. According to the supporters of "intelligent design" they must have drowned in waters. Now that must have been really stupid fish!

In the end, it doesn't really make sense to spend much thought about the "theory of intelligent design". It is not really meant to be a scientific theory. It is only a means for the religious militants to fight science and to discredit it so their "holy truth" can emerge again as the only truth and the ruling force.

*

Religion doesn't only rely on this "scientific" debate to discredit science. Science is also depicted as the source of evil in our world. This line of attack is grouped around the meaning of the word "materialism".

Materialism is originally a quite good description for the scientific approach. Science tries to explain the world and the things that are happening in the world without using divine or any other superhuman intervention, i.e. it relies on material things. The best example is the already mentioned book by the French scientist Pierre-Simon Laplace about the universe. He told the story of the universe and explained how the planets are moving without even mentioning God once. As Laplace said: "Je n'avais pas besoin de cette hypothèse.", I didn't need this hypothesis.

The scientific approach is a materialistic approach as it tries to explain the laws of the world on a purely physical basis. If we would try to explain gravity by referring to the acts of God, then anything would be possible. We could not be sure that gravity always works according to the "inverse square law" (meaning that the force of gravity gets weaker the farther away we are, but the decline is not linear, rather is proportional to the square of the distance). As God is almighty, he could apply a different law for gravity any place and any time. If science should be able to tell us anything about the world, then we have to assume that the world is not constantly modified by a divine force, because then we would not be able to deduce any laws (as we are able to do this and as the laws are the same in different places and at different times, we can assume that the divine intervention, if there should be any, is very marginal).

Science can explain the world without falling back to religion or superstition. Science is purely materialistic. As science freed us from the Dark Ages and the terror and intolerance of religion (on-one would seriously want to live in a country where religion defines the rules – whenever people had the chance they overthrew such an arrogant and intolerant regime), materialism is a highlight of human civilization. It made a lifestyle possible that we have never experienced before. The quality of life improved significantly thanks to science and technology, and the secular and tolerant view about the world enable us to create a democratic society that assures human rights. This never happened while Christian religion dominate life in Europe – and it is not the case today in those countries where the Islamic religion dominates a society. Religion requires autocratic institutions, democracy with its freedom and free thinking is the nemesis of religion.

But that is not how religion sees itself. Religion is intolerant, yet it preaches tolerance; religion is undemocratic, yet it preaches human rights; religion is immoral, yet it preaches moral. If we look at Christian religions today we don't really see that they are intolerant, undemocratic or immoral. That is only because they are not powerful today. When they dominated the society in the Dark Ages, they showed their true face just like some Islamic religious groups show this nasty face of religion today.

Nevertheless, religion pretends to be good, as it pretends it received all its wisdom from God. So science, the great enemy of religion, has to be bad. This means, materialism has to be bad.

Fortunately for religion, there is a second meaning of materialism that "materialized" in the last decades. When materialism originally meant that humans focused on physical rules to explain the world, materialism today rather describes people who only focus their attention on material things, mainly money, instead of immaterial thinks like friendship and love (and religion is love – you can't hate someone if you torture him to help him telling the truth).

Materialism used to be a synonym for science, now it is a synonym for selfishness.

This modified meaning of materialism is now the new line of attack of religion. On first sight, they attack the selfishness of materialism; on second sight they attack science. And once science has been brought down, so they hope, religion can install its regime of love and peace, torture and inquisition, intolerance and arrogance.

Pope Benedict XVI made this clear when he said on a meeting with 400 priests in South Tyrol in the year 2008 that "the real danger for Creation comes from materialism. If you deny God and reduce everything to matter, then there is no basis for a responsibility of man towards God and its Creation". And during the World Youth Day the same year he warned about the "spiritual desert" of materialism and selfishness, while the belief in Jesus Christ can help you to put your life on a solid basis.

The Pope is skillfully mixing both meanings of materialism in his statements. One the one hand, he is against the selfishness of man, on the other hand he attacks science that "reduces everything to matter". The selfishness of man and the materialistic approach of science have nothing to do with each other, yet they are one thing in the eyes of religion.

It is easy to get approval from the listeners if you attack selfishness. That is an immoral behavior, so we are all against it. But then materialism is more, it is trying to reduce everything to matter, to physical laws, explaining the world without referring to the "hypothesis" of God. Once you are emotionally against the selfishness of materialism, it is easy to convince you that the second meaning of materialism is also bad. Physical laws alone cannot describe life, the universe and everything. There has to be more. There has to be God, there has to be religion. Religion is not an add-on to our society, it is its center.

Religion is trying to make its comeback. Religious groups are already quite strong in the USA, and they are getting stronger in Europe. Europeans know from their history what strong religion does to a society – and we can still observe it in some Islamic countries today. Don't let that happen again. Don't let religion defeat science.

The Weak Basis of Religion

The main difference between religion and science is that religion pretends to have all the answers – after all they received their wisdom and information from God – whereas science can only offer to look for the answers.

But we have to be careful: Religion pretends to have all the answers directly from God. How can we be sure that this is really the case? Would you believe someone you meet in the street that he has just met God? Probably you wouldn't. But religion is more than just one person that you meet in the street; it is a large and mighty institution. Millions of people believe that the Bible is the word of God (or at least they joined the club that pretends this). And just because there are so many of them, you can have your doubts if they can really be wrong – or if maybe there is some truth in their statements.

Even if you may have some doubts that the prophets didn't meet God in the end, there is one thing you can be sure of: Even if they have met God and talked to him, they were not able to understand Him correctly.

We already discussed this problem. Everyone has already difficulties understanding a human scientist when he talks about his field of expertise. He is so deep into his science that we will not be able to follow him in every detail. And he is just another human being.

Now imagine a mind so large that it spans the universe, a being so far beyond our imagination that we consider it to be almighty and all-knowing. How should humans be able to understand him? This is simply not possible. Even if the prophets talked to God, they cannot possibly have understood him correctly. This is simply beyond human capabilities.

They act like the three blind men who are trying to describe an elephant that we already mentioned. For the first man the elephant looks like a snake; for the 'second like a wall; and for the third like a tree. And even if these blind men would be able to describe the elephant correctly after some misunderstandings, they will never be able to describe the color of its skin. This is simply beyond the capabilities of a blind man, just like it is beyond human capabilities to understand the mind and sayings of a supernatural being.

If you read the Bible, you find several confirmations for this thesis. You find two contradicting descriptions of the Creation and you find statements about our world (like the statement that the sun is moving around the earth) which are in contradiction to reality. An almighty and all-knowing God should know this. A human mind, however, who tries to understand information that is beyond its understanding, might err and write down nonsensical statements. But then, religion can't pretend it knows the truth because it's written in the Holy Book.

Maybe they even got it wrong when they thought God is almighty, because the existence of an almighty being is full of paradoxes. One of the most famous paradoxes is the following: If God were almighty, then he should be able to create a stone that is so heavy that even he can't lift it.

But if he can't lift it, then he wouldn't be almighty...

Another paradox is the problem of theodicy, the question, why there is evil in the world if it was created by the almighty and absolute Good, i.e. God.

If God is really almighty, then he should be able to create a perfect world, i.e. a world without evil and suffering. As there are evil and sufferings in our world, you wonder if God is really almighty as religion claims.

There have been several efforts to solve this riddle, none of them was convincing. One solution, probably the best known, was offered by the German philosopher Gottfried Wilhelm Leibniz in the 17th century. Leibniz claimed that there simply cannot be a world without evil and sufferings. They are just part of the world like every medal has a second side. All that can be done is to create a world with a minimum of evil and suffering. And this is what God did: He created the best of all possible worlds for us.

In the 18th century, the witty French philosopher Voltaire took this idea as the basis for his novel Candide. In this book, he describes the adventures of Candide, the nephew of a baron from Westphalia, who shares Leibniz optimistic view that we are living in the best of all possible worlds. Candide is enslaved, tortured, experiences the terrible earthquake that almost destroyed Lisbon, and hardly survives. And this, Voltaire asks, is supposed to be the best of all possible worlds?

We will never be able to answer any questions concerning God and his intentions as God, should he exist, is beyond our experience and our capabilities to understand the world.

As this cannot be changed, the best solution for religion is that religion is not put to the test, that nobody asks questions about its truth and only believes what the prophets are telling us.

Religion thus had to make sure that people are not brought into a position where they can ask questions. This was, of course, much easier in those times when religion was in full control than it is today. In former times, people joined the religion at a very early age, in best case even before they could speak and phrase questions. And from that early age on, they were included in the religious activities and religious teachings. Religion was meant to be as normal as learning to walk or talk, as normal as the own parents and neighbors. Religion was meant to be part of your life just like the arm is part of your body – and nobody would think to get rid of its arm (and religion could very well live without those who would).

Secular schools only started in the 19th century, before that, all that our children received were religious teachings. They were in fact not teachings but indoctrinations. People were taught to believe and not to ask questions. So they did and religion blossomed.

In the first centuries of Christian religion, this was even made easier as the Holy Book was only available in Latin, a language that was only spoken by the upper class but rarely by the people. Most people couldn't read anyway, but those who could generally didn't understand Latin, so they were not able to read for themselves what the Bible said. They had to believe that the priests told them the truth which wasn't necessarily the case.

It was Martin Luther's intention to give everybody the chance to judge the actions of the priests and the Holy Church for themselves, when he translated the Bible to German (with other languages following quickly). Now for the first time the people could really see what was mentioned in the Bible – and ask nasty question (like the famous: Why is the Catholic Church amassing wealth if Jesus Christ preached poverty? The answer is simple, as some cynics say: The Church makes the sacrifice to amass all the wealth so the simple people can go to Heaven, for it says in the Bible: "Again I say to you, it is easier for a camel to go through the eye of a needle, than for a rich man to enter the kingdom of God.")

As long as the Bible was written in a cryptic language, as long as all the teaching the people got was controlled by religion, religion was almighty on earth – and the society was intolerant and barbaric.

It needed secular schools to open the eyes of the people and make them see that the strong foundation religion pretends to be standing on is in truth a very weak basis. There is no way to prove that it is correct, and everything we know so far shows us that it isn't. Nevertheless, religion closes its eyes and stubbornly pretends that it is in the possession of the only and divine truth.

This is the source of power for religion, because, in the end, that's all it is about.

Religion and Power

Some people say they get the power to do their daily work from religion. Without their belief they wouldn't be able to help other people in their sufferings as they do. This book is not meant to take away the spiritual basis for these people. If the belief in God gives you strength to do your work, then believe in God. Your personal feelings and beliefs are not the issue.

But religion is not only a personal matter. Religion wants more. Religions became an institution, with administration and rulers. Religion is a mass movement, and mass movements do not act as individuals. In general, they are less rational. And that's where the problem arises.

A mass movement which is told that it is in the possession of the ultimate truth is a danger. It has to be intolerant, is has to be undemocratic and suppress any opposition and critique. Thus, it is the perfect match for dictatorial systems. Religion tells us that they are doing everything for the people. But quickly, every religion is divided into two classes: The believers and the administrators of the belief, the priests and monks. You would say that this shouldn't matter as all are following the words of God, so they are all aligned and don't have different agendas. If only the things were so easy.

Fact is that the believers depend on the administrators of religion. The administrators tell them what to believe; they tell them what to do, what's right and what's wrong. In earlier times, the believers didn't even have the chance to check if the statements of the administrators were correct, as the knowledge about the religion was coded and only available in Latin. Today, the believers have at least the chance to check the reliability and truthfulness of religion. But who does it? Ask your acquaintances about the two stories of Creation in the Bible. You will see astonished faces.

The administrators have the power to steer the people in any direction they want – and for some reason they only take them into these directions that profit themselves. Lying might be a deadly sin, but it seems that the administrators sometimes have to take this difficult path for the higher good of all, i.e. the members of the administration.

A simple life is said to be the goal of Christianity, but the administrators, the churches are almost drowning in wealth. The churches are among the biggest landowners worldwide. They own treasures of an uncountable value. And in Germany, they have the right to collect taxes – almost ten billion Euros each year.

You might say that they use it for charity. Well, the truth is rather that they use it to advertise their charity; the charity itself is mainly paid for by the state. In Germany, we have the situation that the churches own a large number of kindergartens, hospitals and home for the elderly. But they are not paid by the churches; they are almost exclusively paid by the state. The churches only provide the name –

and demand the right to apply their laws within these institutions. So they are only hiring people that share their faith – and fire those that show a behavior which is not compatible with their rules even though it is fully compatible with the laws of society (but we don't have to stress again the intolerance of religion).

It is not a surprise that religion and dictatorship get along well. When religion is strong enough to define the political agenda, it has no problem to take over the spiritual and political work in one person. If religion is weaker, they side with strong authorities, if they were Nazis like in Germany, if they were Franco's dictatorship in Spain or Pinochet's in Chile. If you believe to be in the possession of the ultimate truth, you should also exercise ultimate power – either your own or partnering with a strong hand.

And only if your position is really weak because evil science came up with nasty questions or human rights and democracy, then better run with the pack and pretend to be democratic. Only assure from time to time that your belief is the only true belief that will bring eternal salvation (as the Catholic Church is doing it from time to time).

Religion is built on the understanding that the followers should just do that: follow and don't ask questions. Just believe. This setup is, of course, perfect for any dictatorship. They get easily irate with critique as well. That's why religion gets along well with dictators.

Religion keeps people calm. Its knowledge is not only based on the personal beliefs of a philosopher or dictator, its knowledge is based on the ultimate knowledge of God. If religion tells us how to behave it is not the harassment of a madman, but the moral rules as given to us by God. If people belief, they don't ask questions and will never make a revolution. Religion is the opium for the people, as Karl Marx wrote. It helps either itself or the secular elite it is cooperating with to do as they want, to gather as much wealth as they want, and to lead a life in luxury.

Religion is for the people in the sense that it helps to keep them calm like a flock of sheep, it is not for the people in the sense that it helps to improve their lives. This is reserved for a small elite.

As religion is used by the elite to anaesthetize the people, it is delaying any evolution and technical or social improvement. Even worse: Any civilized improved will be forgotten, as the Christian church showed during the Dark Ages and the Islamic church is showing in some Arab countries where it is bombing civilization back to the Middle Ages.

With its approach to ignore any critique, to make critique even impossible as the truth shall come from an almighty being, religion can exercise an enormous power – and it doesn't always use this power for the good of all. Instead, it favors those that have taken control of the administration of religion, those that changed personal belief into an institution.

Progress, human rights, Enlightenment and democracy can only happen if religion loses its power, if religious belief is only a personal belief and not a political power.

As long as religion is also a political power, it will always try to turn back time to the Dark Ages. We shouldn't let that happen. Don't be fooled by the smiling face of religion, look behind the cover.